THE HOUSE OF WISDOM

ALSO BY JOHN S. DUNNE

The City of the Gods

A Search for God in Time and Memory

The Way of All the Earth

Time and Myth

The Reasons of the Heart

The Church of the Poor Devil

JOHN S. DUNNE

THE HOUSE OF

A PILGRIMAGE

WISDOM

UNIVERSITY OF NOTRE DAME PRESS

Notre Dame/London

248
Du H

Copyright © 1985 by John S. Dunne
First published by Harper & Row, Publishers 1985
University of Notre Dame Press Edition 1993
Published by arrangement with John S. Dunne

Manufactured in the United States of America

Library of Congress Cataloging-in-Publication Data

Dunne, John S., 1929–
    The house of wisdom : a pilgrimage / John S. Dunne
        p. cm.
    Originally published: San Francisco : Harper & Row, c1985
    Includes bibliographical references and index.
    ISBN 0-268-01103-6 (alk. paper)
    1. Spiritual life—Catholic Church. 2. Dunne, John S., 1929–
I. Title.
[BX2350.s.D86   1993]
248—dc20   93-22813
                                                                CIP

to Ayasofya

"my eyes and my heart will be there for all time"
I KINGS 9:3 and II CHRONICLES 7:16*

---

*Here and throughout, unless otherwise indicated, I use the Revised Standard Version (Old Testament 1952 and New Testament 1972).

Contents

Preface

A woman playing before God in the beginning of time, a man crying out to God in the fullness of time, a child playing at the end of time, these are three guises in which I meet the figure of Wisdom on the journey I recount in this book. I call my journey "a pilgrimage," for it takes me to Ayasofya in Istanbul, then to the Rothko Chapel, then to the Meditation Room at the United Nations. I name my book *The House of Wisdom*, thinking of the words "Wisdom has built her house, she has set up her seven pillars."[1]

I set out on my pilgrimage, hoping to learn how to conjoin seeing and feeling, to conjoin knowing and loving—this conjoining is what I am going to call "wisdom." It is what I find in the places I visit, in the things I experience there, in the guises in which I meet the figure of Wisdom. I have come to believe there has been a deep-going separation in our times between knowing and loving, a split in the human spirit, between seeing and feeling too, a split that reaches thus into sense as well, between the two realms that Kant speaks of, "the starry heavens above me and the moral law within me."[2] I have gradually passed in my own life from the one realm to the other; I have gone from living in my mind to living in my heart. That has led me into the darkness of my own heart, divided between the way I am taking in life and the ways I have not taken, and on deeper into the darkness of the human heart as such, the heart's longing in conflict with human misery. Now I think I have to go deeper still, to the place "in my heart where my soul dwells."[3]

When I got into the darkness of my own heart, into my sense of loss in following a way in life and giving up other possible ways (I was writing *The Reasons of the Heart*), I found light in my heart's longing, in the thought of God leading us by the heart, of following the way of the heart's desire. When I went further, though, and got into the darkness of the human heart itself, relating my way to the way of the poor and the hungry and the sorrowful and the outcast (I was writing *The Church of the Poor Devil*), I found I needed two eyes, as it were, to see the human way, an eye for the heart's longing and an eye for human misery. Now as I try to go further still, to find the point of unity behind my binocular vision, I find I need to conjoin my eyes and my heart. I think of the wisdom of God as the eyes and heart of God, as in the words spoken of the Temple, "my eyes and my heart will be there for all time,"[4] and I find myself looking for that place, looking for those eyes, looking for that heart.

I have looked for guidance on my pilgrimage to sayings like that of Kant, "the starry heavens above me and the moral law within me," the words inscribed on his tombstone, or that of Polanyi, "an extreme critical lucidity and an intense moral conscience,"[5] corresponding words but describing the separation that has taken place in our times. Kant's words "the starry heavens above me" make me think of the awakening of my mind in childhood, as I lay outside on a cot on summer nights, gazing up at the stars, how I felt the wonder of existence. His words "the moral law within me" make me think of the awakening of my heart in youth, as I sat on a hilltop and resolved to set out on my spiritual adventure in life. Polanyi's words "an extreme critical lucidity and an intense moral conscience" make me think of lucid and intense moments in manhood when I have felt in myself the separation that has taken place between seeing and feeling, when I have seen my own need for an awakening of soul in knowing and loving.

I have looked also to stories for guidance, especially *The Green Child* by Herbert Read and *The Golden Key* by George Mac-Donald.[6] What draws me to Read's story is the beginning: A man about my own age returns, after a very full life, to the village where he grew up and there he meets a woman, the Green Child, who seems to belong to another world, who is a numinous figure therefore, a guise, I want to think, of the figure of Wisdom. They journey together up the millstream, mysteriously flowing back to its source, and find their way into the world of caves from which she comes, thus passing from air through water into earth. What draws me to MacDonald's story, on the other hand, is the ending, where the man and the woman end up alive rather than dead, although they pass through death. It begins with a boy who finds the Golden Key at the end of a rainbow and a girl who meets him in the enchanted forest at the house of an ageless woman, again a guise, it seems, of the figure of Wisdom. They go on a great journey together, the boy becoming a man and the girl a woman. She goes through water to earth and on to fire, meeting the figure of Wisdom, as it seems to me, in the guise of an old man, a young man, and a child playing, while he goes through death by water to new life, and they meet again, after long being separated, and pass together into the rainbow.

It is meeting the figure of Wisdom that gives these stories their wonder, that gives my own pilgrimage its adventure. Wisdom can seem a figure only of imagination, a personification of God's knowledge and love, as she appears in Proverbs and Sirach and the Wisdom of Solomon. To me, though, she is the reality of that knowledge and love. She is God's eyes and heart— that is how I found her at Ayasofya, the age-old shrine of Holy Wisdom (*Hagia Sophia*), a church for a thousand years, a mosque for five hundred years, and now a museum. She is also the human eyes and heart of Christ, I found at the Rothko Chapel, an unlikely place at first, where the dark murals can seem to reflect only the madness, the terror, and the despair of our times, and yet going from mural to mural as from station to station of the cross, I seemed to see what Christ is seeing, to feel what Christ is feeling. Ultimately she is our eyes and heart, I found in the Meditation Room at the United Nations, as I passed from my eyes to my heart to the place "in my heart where my soul dwells," where God dwells.

What I have found on this pilgrimage is a subtle change, I realize now, in seeing and feeling, in knowing and loving. I think of the change that seems to have come over Aquinas in his last years, that appears in a shift of his view on understanding and wisdom and knowledge and counsel as gifts of the Holy Spirit.[7] Before, he had drawn a clear line between two realms, rather like "the starry heavens above me and the moral law within me," placing understanding and wisdom in the one realm and knowledge and counsel in the other. After, the clear line disappears, and he seems to be caught up himself in a knowing that is loving and a loving that is knowing.

My thanks go to Tim and Gloria Tavis who brought me back

to "my hill of dreams," as I call it here, the hilltop in Austin on which St. Edward's is built, to celebrate their wedding; to Rita Jansen who gave me the idea years ago of going on a pilgrimage someday to Ayasofya; to the Paksoy family for their hospitality in Istanbul, especially Aysen whom I met over here and Aksen and Gulsen, her sisters, whom I met over there; to my friends in Berkeley where I spent a sabbatical year of writing, "a wanderyear of soul," as I call it here, and especially the Holy Cross Fathers with whom I stayed and John and Mary Lee Noonan who let me use their house while they were away in summer; to Mary Sharon Moore who typed my manuscript; to Elizabeth Carr who introduced me to Max Jacob; to Denis and Cathy Nolan and their children whose words I often quote here; to my sister Carrin with whom I stayed in Houston when I was visiting the Rothko Chapel and Claire Wing who came with me to Rothko; to Linda Radler and her sister Kim who let me stay at their place in New York when I was visiting the Meditation Room at the United Nations; and to Maryanne Wolf who invited me to Boston for a panel on nuclear war and, when it was called off, went with me to Hingham, to World's End where my book also ends.

NOTES

1. Proverbs 9:1. It is the passage from which T. E. Lawrence takes his title *Seven Pillars of Wisdom*.
2. Immanuel Kant, *Critique of Practical Reason*, trans. Lewis White Beck (New York: Bobbs-Merrill, 1956), p. 166 ("Two things fill the mind with ever new and increasing admiration and awe, the oftener and more steadily we reflect on them: the starry heavens above me and the moral law within me.").
3. John Donne, Elegy V in *The Poems of John Donne*, ed. Herbert Grierson (London: Oxford University Press, 1960), p. 77. Cf. my discussion below in the last section of Chapter 6.
4. I Kings 9:3 and II Chronicles 7:16.
5. Michael Polanyi, *The Tacit Dimension* (Garden City, N.Y.: Doubleday, 1967), p. 4 ("It seemed to me then that our whole civilization was pervaded by the dissonance of an extreme critical lucidity and an intense moral conscience, and that this combination had generated both our tight-lipped modern revolutions and the tormented self-doubt of modern man outside revolutionary movements.").
6. Herbert Read, *The Green Child* (New York: New Directions, 1948)—this was first published in 1935 and is Read's only novel. George MacDonald,

The Golden Key (New York: Farrar, Straus & Giroux, 1967)—this was originally published in 1867 and is, I believe, MacDonald's finest story.

7. It is a shift that occurs within the *Summa Theologiae* itself, from I–II, q. 68, a. 4 to II–II, q. 8, a. 6 (where Aquinas mentions his change of view on the matter).

1. An Unresolved Symbol

on returning
to my hill of dreams

Almost forty years have passed, and again I sit on this hilltop where I sat when my heart was first enkindled, when I first resolved to set out upon a spiritual adventure. These years have been my days of wandering in the desert, lonely and yet in the company of God, I do believe, a journey with God in time. Now, as I return to my beginning and remember all I hoped, I am ready to hope for more, ready to see the joy of all my desiring.

There is something unresolved in my wandering, something in my loneliness. It is as if I were looking for someone or something I have not found. God has been with me—things are meant, there are signs, the heart speaks, there is a way—but it is as if I were looking for something with God I haven't yet found. It is as if my journey with God in time were "an unresolved symbol," as if I had been wandering these forty years in the desert and were ready now to see the promised land. I am like the man in Herbert Read's story *The Green Child*, going back to his native village after years of life abroad, remembering a strange event that occurred there at the time of his departure, the finding of a woman-child who seemed to belong to another world—"in his mind it had the significance of an unresolved symbol, obscurely connected with his departure, and connected, too, with the inevitability of his return."[1] I want to see now what it would mean to resolve the symbol, to realize it, to pass from symbol to reality.

As I return to my point of departure, I come upon all I have left behind me on my spiritual adventure, all the residue of my life, all my weariness and fear and sadness. I look for someone, as in Read's story, or something, as in George MacDonald's story *The Golden Key*, that points to the wholeness of life and love, someone like the Green Child who can lead me or go with me, something like the Golden Key that can open the door for me into the reality I am seeking. Who is my Green Child? What is my Golden Key? When I look for someone, I think of all the persons I have met. When I look for something, I think of all the discoveries I have made on my journey. When I put the two together, I think of the figure of Wisdom, the personification of God's mind and heart in the Bible, at once someone and something, meeting and enlightening the children of the human race, leading and opening the way into the unknown. Maybe my years of wandering have actually been a pursuit of wisdom, and maybe the figure of Wisdom has been the someone or something I have been seeking without knowing who or what, the person in the persons I have met, the understanding in the discoveries I have made, not a separate person maybe but a person in the persons, not a separate understanding but an understanding in the discoveries. There is enough life and courage and joy here, if I dare believe it, to consume the dregs of my weariness and fear and sadness.

I have now to let Wisdom lead me and go with me, like the Green Child, to open the way before me, like the Golden Key. Yet how am I to go with so indistinct a figure? How am I to follow so unclear an understanding? There is a clue in the story of Solomon. "Ask what I shall give you," God says. "An understanding mind," Solomon replies. "A discerning heart," one could also read.[2] He is asking for a mind according to God's mind, a heart according to God's heart. I have to ask for Wisdom, to prefer her to all else, it seems, and then she will become distinct for me and clear . . .

A PERSON IN THE PERSONS

"Imagination is the beginning of creation," the wise serpent says according to George Bernard Shaw. "You imagine what you desire; you will what you imagine; and at last you create what you will."[3] If you are returning to your beginning, however, as I am doing, you have to go backwards from your creating to your willing, and from your willing to your imagining, and from your imagining at last to your desiring. It is then, when you come to your desire, I expect, you find someone or something you can call Wisdom.

Imagining what you desire, when you are starting out on your spiritual adventure, can mean conceiving a lofty ambition. There is an element of striving in such ambition, of willing what you imagine, and that is what leads to creating what you will. If you return to your beginning, you may feel, as I do, a rekindling of your heart's longing but with all the striving gone out of it. "What do you will?" I have to ask myself, if all the striving is gone, and "What do you imagine?" if lofty ambition is gone, and ultimately "What do you desire?" if without striving and without ambition I can still feel the longing of my heart. Here too I am like the man in *The Green Child*. "To escape from the sense of time, to live in the eternity of what he was accustomed to call 'the divine essence of things'—that was his only desire."[4] Such is my desire, to get away from a sense of time simply passing, to live in time as "a changing image of eternity,"[5] to live in the wonder of existence.

It is to live in the "joy of man's desiring." Those words of the Bach Cantata are like runes to guide me on my quest, as if to say my desiring will lead me to joy, when I go from desiring to imagining to willing to creating, or vice versa, I will come to joy when I come to my desiring, when I come back from creating to willing to imagining to desiring. There is joy in the wonder of existence. I think of the wonder I felt as a boy, lying on my back on a summer night, gazing up at the stars, letting my own imagination be the beginning of creation, as if to impersonate God saying "Let all this exist!" Master Eckhart even says "Existence is God,"[6] thinking no doubt of the wonder, of the awe and the delight. It is the first and main proposition of his teaching. I want to be more cautious here and, instead of saying it is God, only God, say the wonder of existence is a human experience of God. It is a human experience of Wisdom, like the human figure of Jesus:

> Jesu, joy of man's desiring,
> Holy wisdom, love most bright,
> Drawn by Thee, our souls aspiring,
> Soar to uncreated light.[7]

I have come to a simplicity now where I can rest, thinking back to my starting point, to my desiring. I have a journey to go, nevertheless, to come into the joy of my desiring, to come to actually live in the wonder of existence. It is like the journey in Read's story that ends with a man and a woman contemplating the "crystal harmony"[8] of the universe and finally becoming part of the harmony in death. Or better, it is like the journey in MacDonald's story that ends with a man and a woman entering alive into an eternity that has been imaged all along their journey in time.

Dead or alive? That is the question in the end. The answer depends on who or what is wanted in the beginning. I am looking for someone or something that can be the joy of all our desiring, a union or communion with ultimate reality. "We all have within us a center of stillness surrounded by silence,"[9] Dag Hammarskjold says. If union with ultimate reality is seen as a oneness that cannot be experienced, if experiencing something means we are still separated from it, if contemplating the "crystal harmony" of the universe, for instance, means we are not yet part of the harmony, then the story has to end like Read's in my becoming part of the harmony in death. If union with ultimate reality can be a communion with it, on the other hand, if union can be a human experience, that is, if we enter into communion with ultimate reality by entering into our center of stillness, then I may hope to enter alive, as in MacDonald's story, into an eternity that is imaged all along my journey in time. For every time I enter into my own silence and stillness, I am entering into eternity alive.

There in my center of stillness I am hoping to find Wisdom, to find the wonder of existing that Eckhart put into the simple sentence "Existence is God," to find the force of truth that Gandhi put into the equally simple sentence "Truth is God."[10] Such sentences are deceptively simple, easily misunderstood, as if God were a commonplace, when in reality they are the expression of entire lives "illumined by the steady radiance, renewed daily, of a wonder, the source of which is beyond all reason."[11] *What is God for me?* That is the question that must guide me now as I am looking for a person in all the persons I have met, for an understanding in all the discoveries I have made.

Things are meant, there are signs, the heart speaks, there is a way—these are traces I see of God in my life. No doubt, I am desiring and imagining and willing and creating. I am taking things to be meant, watching for signs, waiting for my heart to speak, following the way as it opens before me. Still, I believe I am discovering not just inventing. The persons of my life, if I were just recasting them according to the imagination of my heart, would be like the wonderful folk of the stories I heard as a child. I remember my grandfather telling stories in the evening and the children from the houses around gathering on our front porch to hear him. The folk of stories told aloud "must be the kind of human beings that the human voice can shepherd," as Padraic Colum says, "and the voice cannot shepherd divided, many-mooded, complicated people."[12] I know I myself am one of those people, "divided, many-mooded, complicated." One is always an undefined being to oneself, however well defined one may be to others.

I know the persons of my life too are "divided, many-mooded, complicated," at least to themselves, not "the heroic, sweet, or loving types that are in the world's great stories."[13] Yet they are akin, at the deep center of their being, to the large and heart-whole persons of stories, even as I am akin to the storyteller who tells of his own adventures. When I enter into my center of stillness, I do find a peace, a unity in all my dividedness, a heart's longing in all my many moods, a simplicity in all my complexity. It really is possible, I can see, to love "with all your heart, and with all your soul, and with all your might."[14] The persons I have met appear to me, from this inner standpoint, to belong to my life. A chance meeting of person and person can seem merely chance when it is seen only as the encounter of human purpose and cross-purpose. It can seem more than chance, though, when it is viewed in recollection, when it is seen from a center of silence and stillness. For then purpose and cross-purpose are overshadowed by what seems a greater purpose at work in human lives, by a love that can encompass heart and soul.

Here is where I find a person in all the persons of my life, as if the hearts of all were dwelling in the same solitude. When I am in my center of silence and stillness, I see myself and the persons of my life in terms of our longing for union or communion with ultimate reality. The longing is for what the mystics call "the union of love with God." That union, I realize now, is the something with God that I have been looking for on my own journey in life and haven't yet found. Now I see that the road of my journey is actually "the road of the union of love with god."[15] Somehow it is very illuminating to say this to myself, to say "This is my road!" My encounters with other persons, though on the surface they are only the meeting of "divided, many-mooded, complicated people," appear from this inner place to be the meeting of heart and heart, of longing and longing. "Heart speaks to heart" (*Cor ad cor loquitur*).[16] Something like the figure of Wisdom does come to light here, as if this transcendent longing were a trace of God in our minds and hearts, as if it were an intimation of the mind and heart of God. Mind speaks to mind, heart speaks to heart, soul speaks to soul.

Mind speaks to mind—that is how we meet at first when our longing is simply our mind's desire to understand and not yet our heart's desire to be understood. I met the longing in this shape in my father and in my mother's father, my grandfather who was a storyteller. Both of them had largely educated themselves and both had the enthusiasm for learning that goes with self-education, my father reading and annotating the classics, my grandfather learning all the names of things—the birds and flowers and the trees and the stars. I caught their enthusiasm, as my father would read and I would read, as my grandfather would take me on a walk by a stream and answer all my questions about everything I saw in the water and on the banks. I was like the boy who found the Golden Key, who was called Mossy "because he had a favorite stone covered with moss, on which he used to sit whole days reading."[17] Now, as I look back, I see how my grandfather kindled in me a love of learning about the universe, my father a love of learning about the thoughts of human beings over the ages. I see the enthusiasm, the love itself more than the learning. I see how the love of learning is a loving with the mind, even as in the great commandment to love "with all your mind."

Heart speaks to heart—that is how we meet when our longing

becomes more fully a loving, a longing to know and be known, a longing for intimacy. Here I am like Mossy meeting Tangle (after he has found the Golden Key) and wanting her to come with him on his journey. She does come with him, but they lose touch with each other and find one another again only after they have gone through many changes. There are four stages of love, according to Jung, embodied in four great archetypes of woman: Eve, Helen of Troy, the Madonna, and Sophia or Wisdom.[18] When I envisage Eve, I think simply of the love of man and woman. When I envisage Helen, I think of love and loss. When I envisage the Madonna, I think of the mercy that allows you to recover from loneliness and regret. And when I envisage Sophia, I think of the insight that arises from the experience of love and loss and recovery. I think I must be seeking that insight now as I seek to discover in my own experience the figure of Wisdom. It is an insight that comes of being heart-free and heart-whole, of loving "with all your heart."

Soul speaks to soul—that is how we meet when our hearts are free, when we are willing to walk alone, when our longing has become a longing for God. It is like Mossy and Tangle meeting again at the end when they are about to enter into the rainbow of eternity. There is a dark residue left in the heart when you go through love and loss and recovery. It corresponds to the residue I find I have left behind me on my spiritual adventure, my weariness and fear and sadness. I call the darkness "soul" ("Who can distinguish darkness from the soul?").[19] Somehow I must go through the darkness to the light. I must go through the weariness and the fear and the sadness to the life and the courage and the joy. "Merely to be there was a cure for weariness, fear, and sadness," J. R. R. Tolkien says of Rivendell. I must find in me the place where dark soul becomes luminous, where you can laugh "for heart's ease not for jest,"[21] where you can love "with all your soul."

All ways seem to converge, mind and heart and soul, upon one and the same place within us where "Wisdom has built her house," where "she has set up her seven pillars."[22] There weariness yields to peace of mind, fear to peace of heart, sadness to peace of soul. Or so I want to read those well-known words of Proverbs that gave Lawrence of Arabia the title of his narrative

Seven Pillars of Wisdom. There is adventure in building the house, as in Lawrence's story, but serenity in dwelling there. Or there is adventure in arriving at the house, as in Tolkien's story, but a healing of weariness and fear and sadness in resting there. This is the experience of wisdom, I believe, a peace stabilizing the human spirit, a serenity in adventure, and an adventure in serenity in the journey with God in time.

How are we to find the house of Wisdom? "Some say it is so far, and some say otherwise. It is a strange road, and folk are glad to reach their journey's end, whether the time is long or short."[23] If we try to build the house ourselves, then we are going like Lawrence from desiring to imagining to willing to creating. We are trying to earn "Freedom, the seven-pillared worthy house," as he says, and to think of it as "our work, the inviolate house," but we are in danger like him of disillusionment—"But for fit monument I shattered it, unfinished."[24] If we try instead to discover the house, already built in us by Wisdom herself, then we are going back, as I am doing now, from creating to willing to imagining to desiring. Then it is something that comes to light when mind speaks to mind, when heart speaks to heart, when soul speaks to soul. We find it in ourselves when we find it in one another. It is indeed "Freedom, the seven-pillared worthy house," but it is a freedom of spirit, of mind and heart and soul. "The house is perfected,"[25] as Lawrence says, but in the beginning and by Wisdom herself, not only in the end and by us.

When mind speaks to mind, the house that Wisdom built appears to be "the house of intellect," the lore of the human race, the accumulated learning of the ages. Everything in that lore speaks to us, even when it is spoken in an unknown tongue, even when it is written in an undeciphered language, for we know it is spoken or written by human beings and so we know we have somewhere in our own minds the key to its meaning. I think of all the sayings and the stories I have learned, how they have shaped my living and my thinking. Whenever I study another language and enter into another culture, I encounter new sayings and new stories. I feel like a child, starting all over again, learning everything from the beginning. I find not only parallels with the sayings and the stories I already know. I learn common things I never knew before. Yet they are common, these new things I learn, true of me as well as of the people who speak and write of them. If I think only of their newness to me, I feel a danger of losing the shape that has already been given to my living and my thinking, like Lawrence feeling caught between being English and being Arab—"I had dropped one form and not taken on the other." If I think rather of their truth, how the new things I learn from another people are true of me and mine, how they are common, I feel able to pass over into the other and come back again with new insight to my own.

Here is the Golden Key. It is the capacity we have to pass over to others and come back again to ourselves. We all have the capacity, I believe, but we do not all discover it, come to use it, learn to pass over. Or if we pass over, we are not able to come back to ourselves. "I had dropped one form," Lawrence says, "and not taken on the other . . . with a resultant feeling of intense loneliness in life, and a contempt, not for other men, but for all they do."[26] To get past the loneliness and the contempt, the feelings that accompany cynicism, I find I have to have recourse to faith, to believing in the truth of what I discover, passing over and coming back. I have to acquire the heart of a child, be again the child I was listening to sayings and stories, play with Wisdom herself, "playing" before God:

> I was with him, forming all things,
> And I was delighted every day,
> Playing before him at all times,
>   playing in the world,
> And my delights were to be with
>   the children of men.[27]

When heart speaks to heart, I begin to find delight "with the children of men" instead of "intense loneliness in life, and a contempt, not for other men, but for all they do." Then the house that Wisdom built appears, as in this passage from Proverbs, to be the whole earth, the home of the human race. There is a deep loneliness, to be sure, that is part of being human, a longing for intimacy, but it begets contempt and cynicism only when there is no hope of fulfilling the heart's longing. Whenever heart speaks to heart, there is hope, there is fulfillment, for we

are meeting then where we are most alone. "From the heart—
may it go to the heart" (*Von Herzen—Möge es zu Herzen gehen*),[28]
Beethoven writes over the Kyrie Eleison of his Mass in D. If we
speak from the heart, if we speak out of the deep loneliness of
the human condition, even out of the longing for God, as in
Beethoven's Mass, then it may go to the heart. I feel the deep
loneliness, for example, at the prospect of a journey alone,
especially a journey alone in a foreign country. Heart speaks to
heart for me when I find another who knows this loneliness,
who feels alone too on our human journey through time to
eternity, who can be with me in my aloneness.

Here, for me, is the Green Child. She is the figure who is
with me when I am alone, a paradoxical idea, for "alone" means
"no one with me." She corresponds to Eve, to Helen, to the
Madonna, but especially and finally to Sophia, the figure of
Wisdom. I meet Sophia, it seems, whenever I meet someone
who knows loneliness. I meet her, as in Read's story, on my way
back to my beginning, on the journey into myself and beyond
myself. I meet her when something comes "from the heart" and
goes "to the heart." In the beginning, according to the story of
Adam and Eve, God created man alone (the Koran even has
God call man "him whom I created alone"), but then God said,
"It is not good that the man should be alone,"[29] and God created
woman. It is when I go back to that original aloneness in myself
that I find the meaning of the figure who is Eve, Helen, the
Madonna, Sophia, and it is when I meet that original aloneness
in another that I actually meet her. To know human aloneness,
I begin to realize now, is to know the divine oneness; it is to be
"alone with the Alone" (*solus cum solo*);[30] and that, I can see, is
a taste of the Wisdom that was with God in the beginning.

When soul speaks to soul, I learn what it truly means to be
"alone with the Alone." Now at last the house that Wisdom built
appears to be "the house of God." Self appears when I am
alone; soul appears when I am unalone, when I am "alone with
the Alone." Being "with the Alone," it seems, is the essence of
soul. It is true, soul is dark until our hearts are free, until we
are willing to walk alone, until our heart's longing has become
consciously a longing for God. As we become conscious and
willing, though, the darkness of the soul becomes, according to

the title of a classic of mysticism, "the cloud of unknowing, in the which a soul is oned with God."[31] What begins in the love of learning as a meeting of minds, becomes in the process of passing over and coming back a meeting of hearts, and ends in the state of being "oned with God" as a meeting of souls. I think of my experience of traveling abroad, how it begins in a desire to learn the language and the ways of other peoples, their culture, their lives, their religion, how it becomes for me an encounter with other persons where something comes "from the heart" and goes "to the heart," and how it ends when I have come back home and am trying to assimilate what has happened to me in a sense of returning to the source of my being.

Here is the way of my journey with Sophia, the figure of Wisdom, like that of Olivero and Siloen in *The Green Child*, or that of Mossy and Tangle in *The Golden Key*. I have to go with her, as with Siloen, through water to earth or, as with Tangle, through water to earth to fire to the rainbow. There is the way of the mind, the way of the heart, and the way of the soul. If being "oned with God" is not an experience, if "the mere fact that the individual *feels* his presumed unity with God as a personal experience indicates that he is still separated from God,"[32] then the journey has to end in death like that of Olivero and Siloen, their bodies becoming part of the "crystal harmony" of earth like stalactites and stalagmites. If union with God can be an experience of communion with God, on the other hand, then the journey can end in life like that of Mossy and Tangle, passing alive into the rainbow bridging heaven and earth.

AN UNDERSTANDING IN THE DISCOVERIES

"All was plain," it seemed to Tangle when she came to the heart of the earth, "she understood it all, and saw that everything meant the same thing, though she could not have put it into words."[33] Everything meant the same thing, everything, that is, that she had heard and learned on her journey. Passing over to others and coming back to myself, as I am doing on my own journey, I discover more and more about others, more and more about myself. If I look for an understanding in all the discoveries I have made, as if "everything meant the same thing," I come to an understanding of understanding itself, of passing over and coming back, of what it is to understand. I come to "a knowing of knowing."[34] That phrase, from Aristotle to Hegel, has served as a definition of God. There is something lacking in it, nevertheless, as appears in Aristotle's conclusion that the knowing of knowing must know only itself and nothing else since nothing else would be worthy of its attention. My own experience of God, that things are meant, that there are signs, that the heart speaks, that there is a way, seems to point rather toward a knowing that reaches beyond itself, that knows us and our lives and our universe. The understanding that is there in my discoveries, I guess, must reach beyond itself too, must reach to the things, the signs, the heart, the way. What God is for me must be there in that understanding, a knowing of knowing and unknowing.

It is because of the unknowing, I suspect, that "she could not have put it into words again," because the understanding that she came to, that I must come to, reaches to the realm not only of mind but also of heart and soul. Really there are three realms here, mind and heart and soul: There is knowing, and there is being known, and there is unknowing. "Thoroughly understand what it is to understand," Bernard Lonergan says, extolling the power of the knowing of knowing, "and not only will you understand the broad lines of all there is to be understood but also you will possess a fixed base, an invariant pattern, opening upon all further developments of understanding."[35] Understand what it means to be understood by another person, I must say, go from knowing to being known, and you will begin to understand hearts, to understand the heart's desire to be understood, to see how all human hearts dwell in the same solitude. Understand how we are dark to our own understanding, moreover, go on from knowing and being known to unknowing, and you will begin to understand souls, to see how in "the cloud of unknowing" a soul is united with God.

Wisdom begins in knowing, it seems, goes through being known, and ends in unknowing. It begins in the realm of the mind, passes into that of the heart, and ends in that of the soul. It is when I pass into the realm of the heart that I see things are meant and there are signs and the heart speaks and there is a way, for the things that enter a life appear to belong to the life only in the light of the heart's desire, and the heart speaks when the heart's desire is felt so as to illumine circumstances, and the way appears as the road of the heart's desire. When I come to the point of seeing "that everything meant the same thing," however, the things happening, the signs pointing, the heart speaking, the way leading, and yet "could not have put it into words again," I enter the realm of the soul. For if everything means "the same thing," it means God. "The breadth of all growing things which rest along the pathway bestows the world," Martin Heidegger says. "In what remains unsaid in their speech is—as Eckhart, the old master of letter and life, says—God, only God."[36]

How am I speaking of it if I "could not have put it into words again"? There is a way of speaking of God without actually mentioning God, as when I say "things are meant, there are signs, the heart speaks, there is a way." It is possible, as Tolkien does, to tell a whole story in this fashion without ever mentioning God. Once I mention God, as I am doing now, I am trying, perhaps unwisely, to say "what remains unsaid in their speech," to give words to what can be fully expressed only by the Word.

"My name, and yours," Ursula Le Guin says, "and the true name of the sun, or a spring of water, or an unborn child, all are syllables of the great word that is very slowly spoken by the shining of the stars."[37] The Logos, "the great word," is connected somehow with Sophia, the figure of Wisdom. I meet Sophia, I have been saying, when mind speaks to mind, when heart speaks to heart, when soul speaks to soul. I meet her, that is, when "syllables of the great word" are spoken. Now in a meeting of minds I have to pass over from what is said to what is unsaid, if I am really to understand another person. Say I am hearing someone's own story. I have to pass over from the events of the life to the person who is living the life, to whom the events are happening, I have to pass over from the story to the storyteller, if I am really to understand the life and the significance of the events, if I am to learn a person's "true name."

When I do pass over to another person, I do not come straightaway to see the other in a new light. I come rather to see what the other sees and feel what the other feels. That is what passing over is, entering into the standpoint of another, seeing with another's eyes, feeling with another's heart. It is like going from the northern to the southern hemisphere and seeing the stars in new constellations in the night sky. There are stars that can be seen only in the northern sky, as the North Star itself and the constellations of the Big and the Little Dipper, and there are those that can be seen only in the southern sky, as in the constellation of the Southern Cross, and there are those that can be seen in both, as the constellation of Orion the Hunter. Thus, when I travel to the southern hemisphere, I come to see stars and constellations I have never seen before, although I see also the continuity and the overlap of the northern and southern sky. So too, when I pass over into another's life, I see events and patterns of events I have never seen before, although I see a continuity and an overlap of my life and the other's. I come by traveling to see the whole sky over time and all the stars that are visible to the naked eye. So too, I come by passing over to see human existence as a whole and all the things that belong to a human life.

It is in seeing life as a whole that I meet Sophia, that I encounter the Logos. I see really two things: (1) that it is possible to pass over from the standpoint of one's own life to that of another person, and (2) that God, though called by a different name in every standpoint, as Eckhart saying "Existence is God" and Gandhi saying "Truth is God," is nevertheless one and the same. I meet Sophia, I encounter the Logos when I have a feeling for the continuity of standpoints, when I see the continuity. What I am thinking of here is the deep continuity that allows one human being to understand another. It is a meeting of minds, not in our conception of ultimate reality but in our experience of a reality that is above and beyond all our conceptions of it.

I think of seeing the Bedouin pray when I was traveling in the Sinai desert, especially once at sunset when I came up to a Bedouin village on the Gulf of Akaba that was called Dahab. I saw an old man facing southeast across the water as is the custom in Muslim prayer, paying no attention to me or the people I was with or the noise we were making. I saw him facing not just toward Mecca and the Islamic conception of God as Allah but facing toward that ultimate reality that is above and beyond all our conceptions of it. I felt what Charles de Foucauld must have felt when he saw the Bedouin praying in the Sahara. "Islam shook me deeply . . . seeing such faith," he says, "seeing people living in the continual presence of God, I came to glimpse something bigger and more real than worldly occupations."[38] It is true, I was led, he was led to Christianity rather than to Islam. I passed over, he passed over to the Bedouin praying in the desert, but we both came back again to find that reality, to find the God who exists in the context of our own lives.

Now in coming back to the standpoint of our own lives, we can come to a meeting of hearts. Say I tell another person the story of my own life, including, for instance, the story I have just been telling about seeing the Bedouin pray in the Sinai. Say we share a feeling of dissatisfaction at living for a limited goal, come to "glimpse something bigger and more real than worldly occupations." Say we are both moved deeply by seeing faith, by "seeing people living in the continual presence of God." We come then to a meeting of hearts, to a sense of understanding and being understood in our heart's desire. We come at the same time, as Foucauld himself did, to a feeling for solitude, even if we do not pursue it as he did in a solitary life as a hermit in the desert. We come together in understanding and being understood at the very moment we seem to be moving apart into solitude, knowing our hearts dwell where God dwells.

There is a spiritual torpor and apathy, however, that envelops and conceals the heart's desire for God when we are alone and do not want to be alone. It was called *acedia* by the solitaries of the desert in ancient times. I recognize it in the weariness and fear and sadness I left behind me on my spiritual adventure and am meeting now again in returning to my beginning. If we become willing to walk alone, to live in the solitude where all human hearts dwell, I can guess, the torpor and apathy will pass, will yield to the taste of the heart's desire. Simply knowing the solitude of our hearts, as I do now, knowing our hearts can meet in solitude, knowing our hearts dwell where God dwells is not enough. There has to be a willingness to walk alone with God, I can see, to ask God for "an understanding mind," as

Solomon did, for "a discerning heart," to say, as Thomas Aquinas did, "Lord, nothing but you." I gaze at Sassetta's painting, "The Vision of Saint Thomas Aquinas"; I write down the words of Aquinas like a motto, as Samuel Johnson did in his diary, *Nullum, Domine, nisi teipsum*;[39] but I have yet to come to such wisdom, to know what is enough for me, to know God is enough for me.

Here again I meet Sophia, I encounter the Logos. Wisdom, I can see, is in knowing what is enough for you, in knowing God is enough for you. I know and I don't know. Yet I know of a way to wisdom. It can be seen in the sequence of figures: Eve, Helen, the Madonna, Sophia. The key figure is the next to last, the Madonna who embodies the divine mercy. The way to wisdom is mercy, I believe, not sheer renunciation of everyone and everything other than God. There is a choice, to be sure, between going forward toward Sophia and going backward toward Helen and Eve. So there is a renunciation, there is a letting go. Yet mercy is the way. One can't go directly to wisdom from being caught up in having (Eve) and not having (Helen). One comes by way of mercy. I can ask God for mercy even when I am not pure enough of heart to ask for wisdom. I can meditate on mercy:

> The quality of mercy is not strained:
> It droppeth as the gentle rain from heaven
> Upon the place beneath. It is twice blest;—
> It blesseth him that gives, and him that takes.
> 'Tis mightiest in the mightiest: it becomes
> The thronèd monarch better than his crown.
> His sceptre shows the force of temporal power,
> The attribute to awe and majesty,
> Wherein doth sit the dread and fear of kings;
> But mercy is above this sceptred sway:
> It is enthroned in the heart of kings,
> It is an attribute to God himself;
> And earthly power doth then show likest God's
> When mercy seasons justice.[40]

As I meditate on mercy, my mind, my heart is carried to wisdom, for mercy is compassion, and compassion is understanding, and understanding is wisdom. Indeed the words in praise of mercy are like the words in praise of wisdom, as if Shakespeare were echoing here a passage from the Bible. There is a blessing in the give and take of mercy ("It blesseth him that gives, and him that takes.") that leads from mercy to wisdom, from "Blessed are the merciful, for they shall obtain mercy" to "Blessed are the pure in heart, for they shall see God."[41] I see it happening for me in my experience of passing over to others and coming back to myself, for passing over involves entering into sympathy with others, letting compassion become understanding, and coming back involves coming to a new insight into my own life, letting understanding become wisdom. Still, the understanding I come to in passing over is always partial—I enter into the standpoint of another but do not actually become the other. So the wisdom I arrive at in coming back is partial too—I come to an insight into my heart's desire, but there is still a residue of darkness in my heart.

Now in the darkness of our hearts, I may still hope, we can come to a meeting of souls. I know and I don't know that God is enough for me. My knowing is my insight into my heart's desire; my unknowing is the darkness of my heart. If I may take my unknowing to be "the cloud of unknowing, in the which a soul is oned with God," then I may hope to find God in the darkness of my heart, as if the residue of my life were not simply weariness and fear and sadness but something in me that is weary and fearful and sad, something that is capable of life and courage and joy. That something is soul. Somehow mercy is the cure, I know, as I continue to show mercy in passing over to others, as I continue to obtain mercy in coming back to myself, and the blessing at work in mercy, I think, is turning my soul into "a mercy seat,"[42] a throne of God, a place of divine access, where loneliness gives way to life and light and love.

I find the place where soul becomes pure and simple, that is, where dark soul becomes luminous, when I find the place of mercy in myself. I find the place, even though soul is still dark to me. I recognize the place, as if it were home. Here is the place of purgation and illumination and union. It is like the origin of a coordinate system, the intersection of the axes of Cartesian coordinates. It is the place where I start in passing over to others and the place where I end in coming back to myself. Indeed passing over is like a transformation of coordinates, as in Einstein's theory of relativity, a going over from one to another set of coordinates, from one to another origin. When I become aware of this place, the origin, the zero point of my own life, and I pass over to the same point in another life, there is a meeting of souls. It is the place that Hammarskjold is talking about, I suppose, when he says, "We all have within us a center of stillness surrounded by silence." It is what Master Eckhart calls "the ground of the soul" or "the spark of the soul" or "the essence of the soul," the point at which the soul becomes one with God.

Here is where the Word is spoken, where the Logos comes to birth in the soul. "God in the conception and guise of truth enters the understanding," Master Eckhart says. "He enters the will in the conception and guise of good; but through his naked essence, which is above any name, he enters and penetrates into the naked essence of the soul, which also has no name of its own."[43] God enters the mind, God enters the heart, God enters the soul, I could say in the language I have been using. The Word is spoken when I realize that God in "his naked essence" is "above any name." The Logos is born when God "enters and penetrates into the naked essence of the soul." The oneness of God and the soul appears when I realize that "the naked essence of the soul" too "has no name of its own." There is an affinity, I realize, between the ultimate reality that is above and beyond all our conceptions of it and the origin, the zero point of my own life.

What is happening here is analogous to the Madonna giving birth to the Child. I take the way of mercy to wisdom, and it leads me into my own center of stillness. There the Word is spoken to me, the Logos comes to birth in me. It is as if the Logos or Word that is told of in the prologue of John's Gospel, "In the beginning was the Word," came to birth in time, "and the Word became flesh and dwelt among us,"[44] and now comes to birth in the soul. It is as if "the eternal birth,"[45] as Master Eckhart calls it, were always taking place in eternity, but takes place in historic time at the coming of Jesus Christ, and is taking place now in the time of my life. The image of the Madonna and Child is the key, suggesting that mercy gives birth, that what happens at the birth of Christ in Bethlehem happens also in me, "The hopes and fears of all the years are met in thee tonight,"[46] that light is born in me, "the everlasting light," shining in the dark of my unknowing hopes and fears.

My hopes and my fears are the core of my unknowing. My hopes maybe are vain, my fears groundless, but they keep me from letting God be my only hope and fear. Coming to wisdom by way of mercy, as I am doing, rather than by way of disillusionment, I come to the thought of hopes and fears being "met" rather than being simply vain and groundless. To be met is to be taken care of, I am thinking, by a God who cares for all, as when you turn over all your cares to God in prayer. It is one thing simply to let go of all your concerns; it is another to turn them over to God. For in simply letting go you are becoming free by no longer caring, but in turning your hopes and fears over to God you become heart-free and yet still care. Say I have secret hopes, of meeting someone who will change my life and make me a new man, secret fears, of dying without having really lived, hopes and fears for all the persons who belong to my life and enter into it, for myself in relation to them. Say I turn them all over to God, though I know my hopes maybe are vain, my fears groundless. "I have no hope; I have no fear; I am free,"[47] Nikos Kazantzakis says in words inscribed on his tombstone. I hope still, but I hope in God; I fear still, but I fear God; I am free, not of care but of the burden of care.

I seem nearer to God now, to knowing what is enough for me, to knowing God is enough for me, for I am seeing God no longer as Someone or Something set over against everyone and everything belonging to my life but rather as the One who encompasses all. Yet what am I expecting of God, I ask myself, when I turn everything over? No doubt, I am expecting things entering my life will belong to it and things belonging to it will enter it. I am expecting things will be meant; that is, there will be signs, the heart will speak, there will be a way. What then is God for me? What is enough for me? *Life and light and love*, I will say, as in John's Gospel and Epistle, thinking of the way of the mind (light), the heart (love), the soul (life), thinking the life in us is God's, as in the sentence "God dwells in you," the light is God's, as in Newman's prayer "Lead, Kindly Light," the love is God's, as in the words of the old man to Lawrence of Arabia, "The love is from God and of God and towards God."[48]

I have found no sentence, however, quite as simple as Eckhart's "Existence is God" or Gandhi's "Truth is God." Maybe that is because I am not yet as pure and simple as they were, because I know and I don't know what is enough for me. If we say God is "that greater than which nothing can be conceived,"[49] as Anselm does, then to say "Existence is God" is to say nothing can be conceived greater than existence, I can see, and to say "Truth is God" is to say nothing can be conceived greater than truth. Far-reaching consequences arise, I can see too, as when Gandhi says, "To see the universal and all-pervading Spirit of Truth face to face one must be able to love the meanest of creation as oneself."[50] It is like the rabbinical story of a student asking "In olden days there were men who saw the face of God. Why don't they anymore?" and the rabbi answering "Because nowadays no one can stoop so low."[51]

To come to this myself, to see the universal and all-pervading Spirit of Truth, to love the meanest of creation as myself, to stoop low enough to see God, I must follow the way I have found, the way of mercy. It is by passing over to others and coming back again to myself that I will find "that greater than which nothing can be conceived" in everyone and everything I meet in my life. It is by way of mercy that I will come to the purity and simplicity of wisdom, as if Sophia were a transfiguration of the Madonna, as if the Word, when spoken to us, were something as simple as "I am."

When I think of God saying "I am" to Moses from the burning bush, when I think of the "I am" sayings of Jesus in John's Gospel, I begin to see the connection among the three great metaphors that John uses, life and light and love.[52] It is when I pass over to the origin, the zero point of another life, where the other can say "I am," and come back again to that of my own life that mind speaks to mind, heart speaks to heart, soul speaks to soul. Now I begin to be indeed like Tangle at the heart of the earth, seeing "that everything meant the same thing, though she could not have put it into words again." Or if I do put it into words again, it will be the words "I am." Passing over to others and coming back again to myself, I begin to see the connection between the zero point of my own life and that of every other life. I see a connection between "I am" as I say it myself and "I am" as every other person says it, between "I am" as a human being can say it and the great "I am" that is the Word of God. As I go over to the origin of other lives and come back again to that of my own, I am on my way, it seems, to oneness with God, to being at the origin of the universe. I am on "the road of the union of love with God."

I am not simply making "the turn to the subject," the turn that occurred in modern thought when Descartes made "I am" his starting point. I am going over from that point in myself to that same point in others, coming back to it again, in myself, and going on to find a person in the persons I meet, an understanding in the discoveries I make. It is as if the center of stillness I find we each have within us were the center of a sphere that is infinite, a sphere whose center is everywhere, whose circumference is nowhere.[53] I don't mean to interpret this in the Hindu way, "God dwells in you as you,"[54] but only in the Christian way, "God dwells in you." As I pass over from my own center to that of others, nevertheless, and come back again to my own, I realize more and more that I am coming to a center that is everywhere.

It is the distance I have to cross, passing over and coming back, the distance I have to travel, going to the center, that keeps me to saying "God dwells in you" rather than "God dwells in you as you." Seeing the distance is like feeling the immensity of the universe. It is like seeing the giant redwood trees. "It was very healing to be near them and in the forest," a friend wrote to me. "The fatigue of the days dropped from us and we were small creatures again in a big world made by God." There is a fatigue that comes of living always in our own standpoint without passing over, where the world is small and we are large, where it is up to us to create and sustain and govern the world. It is healing to enter into the greater world that encompasses the smaller, where things are no longer in our hands, God's world like a larger sphere, even an infinite sphere, concentric with the smaller one of the days. Something new begins in us. We are somehow more alive and awake than we have been for a long time. God is starting something, it seems, that we shall see.

"Lead, Kindly Light," if I may use those words myself, is Yes to what has begun in me, Yes to being alive and awake, Yes to what God is starting . . .

I have loved God more than I thought, I am beginning to realize, loved without realizing I was loving, much as you can be in love, man and woman, without realizing it. My journey, to put it most simply, is to go from infatuation to wisdom—that is my road now, "the road of the union of love with God." I have to go from infatuation, from being caught up in everyone and everything I meet, by way of mercy, by passing over to others and coming back to myself, to wisdom, to knowing what is enough for me, to knowing God is enough for me. I come to wisdom, though, as I realize it is God I love, as I realize the love in my life really is "from God and of God and toward God." It makes a difference, I can see, to realize you love God. It makes a difference in the love itself. It is like saying you are in love—the love becomes conscious and willing. To love God is indeed to be in love.

NOTES

1. Herbert Read, *The Green Child* (New York: New Directions, 1948), p. 27.
2. Kings 3:5 and 9.
3. George Bernard Shaw, *Back to Methuselah*, quoted by Padraic Colum, *Storytelling New and Old* (New York: Macmillan, 1968), p. 23.
4. Read, *The Green Child*, p. 12.
5. Plato, *Timaeus* 37d (my translation).
6. Master Eckhart, *Parisian Questions and Prologues*, trans. Armand A. Maurer (Toronto: Pontifical Institute of Medieval Studies, 1974), pp. 85–86. The Latin sentence is *Esse est Deus*. Cf. Master Eckhart, *Die lateinischen Werke*, ed. Konrad Weiss, vol. 1 (Stuttgart: W. Kohlhammer, 1964), p. 38.
7. Johann Sebastian Bach, "Jesu, Joy of Man's Desiring" (from Cantata 147, "Herz und Mund und Tat und Leben," 1716), ed. Richard G. Appel (New York: Oliver Ditson, 1933). The words are a free translation, done for the Church Music Society, of verses of Martin Jahn's "Jesu, meiner Seelen Wonne" (1661).
8. Read, *The Green Child*, p. 194.
9. Dag Hammarskjold, his leaflet for the United Nations Meditation Room, "A Room of Quiet" (New York: United Nations, 1971), opening sentence.
10. Cf. Mahatma Gandhi, *An Autobiography: The Story of My Experiments with Truth*, trans. Mahadev Desai (Boston: Beacon, 1968), pp. xiii–xiv. ("There are innumerable definitions of God, because His manifestations are innumerable. They overwhelm me with wonder and awe and for a moment

stun me. But I worship God as Truth only.") and p. 503 ("My uniform experience has convinced me there is no other God than Truth.").

11. Dag Hammarskjold, *Markings*, trans. Leif Sjoberg and W. H. Auden (New York: Knopf, 1964), p. 56.
12. Colum, *Storytelling New and Old*, p. 4.
13. Ibid, p. 14.
14. Deuteronomy 6:5. Cf. also Matthew 22:37, Mark 12:30, and Luke 10:27 that add "and with all your mind."
15. Saint John of the Cross, *Dark Night of the Soul*, trans. E. Allison Peers (Garden City, N.Y.: Doubleday, 1959), p. 34.
16. John Henry Newman's motto on his cardinal's coat of arms. He seems to have derived it from Saint Francis de Sales (*cor cordi loquitur*), as quoted in his *Idea of a University* (London: Longmans, 1886), p. 410.
17. George MacDonald, *The Golden Key* (New York: Farrar, Straus & Giroux, 1967), p. 30.
18. C. G. Jung, "The Psychology of the Transference," in *The Practice of Psychotherapy* (vol. 16 of his *Collected Works*), trans. R. F.C. Hull (New York: Pantheon, 1954), p. 174.
19. W. B. Yeats, "A Dialogue of Self and Soul," in *Collected Poems* (New York: Macmillan, 1956), p. 230.
20. J. R. R. Tolkien, *The Lord of the Rings* (London: Allen & Unwin, 1969), p. 241.
21. Ibid., p. 677.
22. Proverbs 9:1.
23. Tolkien, *The Lord of the Rings*, p. 204.
24. T. E. Lawrence, *Seven Pillars of Wisdom* (Harmondsworth, England: Penguin and Jonathan Cape, 1971), p. 9.
25. Ibid, p. 601.
26. Ibid, p. 30.
27. Proverbs 8:30-31. (Douay-Challoner Version with slight modifications).
28. Ludwig van Beethoven, *Missa Solemnis* (Opus 123 in D major) (London: Ernest Eulenberg, 1902), p. 1.
29. Genesis 2:18. Cf. Arthur J. Arberry, *The Koran Interpreted* (New York: Macmillan, 1973), 2:310 (Sura 74:11).
30. Cf. John Henry Newman on *solus cum solo* in his *Apologia* (London: Longmans, 1875), pp. 196f.
31. Cf. *The Cloud of Unknowing*, trans. Clifton Wolters (Baltimore: Penguin, 1976), p. 36.
32. Ira Progoff, in the introduction to his translation of *The Cloud of Unknowing* (New York: Dell, 1957), p. 37.
33. MacDonald, *The Golden Key*, p. 59.
34. Aristotle, *Metaphysics*, XII, 1074b34 (my translation). Hegel ends his *Philosophy of Mind*, trans. William Wallace (Oxford: Clarendon, 1894), p. 97 by quoting the related passage 1072b18-30.
35. Bernard Lonergan, *Insight* (London: Longmans, 1961), p. xxviii.
36. Martin Heidegger, "The Pathway," trans. Thomas F. O'Meara, in *Listening*, vol. 2 (Dubuque, Iowa: Aquinas Institute, 1967), p. 89.
37. Ursula Le Guin, *A Wizard of Earthsea* (Berkeley, Calif.: Parnassus, 1968), p. 185.
38. Charles de Foucauld, quoted in *Silent Pilgrimage to God* by a Little Brother of Jesus, trans. Jeremy Moiser (Maryknoll, N.Y.: Orbis, 1975), p. 15.
39. Cf. Aquinas's own discussion of *acedia* as a spiritual sadness in his *Summa*

Theologiae, II–II, q. 35 (I use the Marietti edition, Rome and Turin, 1950). Sassetta's painting (1423–26) is in the Pinacoteca at the Vatican, #71 in *The Vatican Collections* (New York: Metropolitan Museum of Art, 1982), p. 139. Samuel Johnson's diary entry is for September 8, 1783, in *Diaries, Prayers, and Annals* (vol. 1 of *The Yale Johnson*), ed. E. L. McAdam, Jr. with Donald and Mary Hyde (New Haven: Yale University Press, 1958), p. 364 (cf. also note on p. 365).

40. Shakespeare, *The Merchant of Venice*, Act IV, scene 1, lines 180-193. The line "It droppeth . . ." seems to echo Sirach 35:20, and the lines about kings seem to echo Seneca, *De Clementia*, I, Chapter 19, but I see a general likeness between the praise of mercy here and the praise of wisdom in Proverbs, Sirach, and The Wisdom of Solomon.
41. Matthew 5:7 and 8.
42. Exodus 25:17.
43. Eckhart, *Defensio*, IX, 51, trans. Raymond Blakney in *Master Eckhart* (New York: Harper, 1941), p. 301.
44. John 1:1 and 14.
45. Cf. the first four sermons in Blakney, *Master Eckhart*, pp. 95–124.
46. From "O Little Town of Bethlehem" by Phillips Brooks, in his *Christmas Carols* (New York: Dutton, 1903), p. 10.
47. Cf. Kimon Friar in the introduction to his translation of Kazantzakis, *The Saviours of God* (New York: Simon & Schuster, 1969), p. 36.
48. Newman's prayer can be found in *A Newman Reader*, ed. Francis X. Connelly (Garden City, N.Y.: Image, 1964), pp. 74–75. Cf. my discussion of it in my book *The Church of the Poor Devil* (New York: Macmillan, 1982), pp. 54–55. Lawrence tells the story of his encounter with the old man in *Seven Pillars of Wisdom*, p. 364. Cf. my discussion of the old man's words about "the love" in my book *The Reasons of the Heart* (New York: Macmillan, 1978), pp. 1–3.
49. I am putting together two phrases here that Anselm uses to describe God in his *Proslogion*, Chapter 2, *aliquid quo nihil majus cogitari possit* and *id quo majus cogitari non potest*. Cf. *Sancti Anselmi Opera Omnia*, ed. F. S. Schmitt, vol. 1 (Edinburgh: Nelson, 1946), p. 101.
50. Gandhi, *An Autobiography*, p. 504.
51. The story is recounted by Jung in his autobiography, *Memories, Dreams, Reflections*, ed. Aniela Jaffe, trans. Richard and Clara Winston (New York: Vintage, 1963), p. 355.
52. Exodus 3:14 ("Say this to the people of Israel, 'I AM has sent me to you.'"); John 8:24, 28, 58; 18:5–6 ("I am" sayings of Jesus where there is no predicate following). Cf. John 4:24 ("God is spirit," cf. John 6:63 on "spirit and life"), 1 John 1:15 ("God is light"), and 1 John 4:8 ("God is love"), and also John 1:4 ("In him was life, and the life was the light of men.").
53. Cf. my discussion of the metaphor of the infinite sphere at the end of my book *The Way of All the Earth* (New York: Macmillan, 1972), p. 232.
54. "God dwells in you as you" is Swami Muktananda's way of putting the traditional *tat tvam asi* ("You are that") of the Upanishads (cf. my discussion in *The Way of All the Earth*, pp. 219–220). Cf. Muktuananda's autobiography, *The Play of Consciousness* (San Francisco: Harper & Row, 1978), p. xxxiv ("May our lives be the play of universal Consciousness!").

2. Holy Wisdom

on coming into
Ayasofya in Istanbul

I wonder if human eyes can meet the eyes of God, if the human heart can endure the heart of God. This place, dedicated to Holy Wisdom (*Hagia Sophia*), is a place to pray like Solomon for "an understanding mind," for "a discerning heart," a place like the Temple of Solomon—I can feel the power of it—where God has promised "my eyes and my heart will be there for all time."[1]

A church for almost a thousand years, a mosque for nearly five hundred years, and now a museum, it is still, I want to think, a place of prayer and pilgrimage. I have come here, at any rate, on a kind of pilgrimage, a quest of wisdom, hoping to encounter Holy Wisdom with my eyes and my heart, to see with my eyes the light and the shadows, the walls and the space here, to feel in my heart the presence, not only my own and that of others who come, to know what it is like being here, but more, to feel the divine presence, if I can, to feel even the presence of Holy Wisdom herself. I will call her Ayasofya at times now instead of Sophia, using the Turkish name of the place, Ayasofya, derived from the Greek name, Hagia Sophia, as if it were the name of a person. I am thinking of what a young Turkish woman said to me, seeing me spending hours here every day, as I have been doing, walking around inside, praying and thinking and writing. "You are in love with Ayasofya," she said. I think she is right. I have come here, trying to go from quest and loss and recovery to wisdom, from Eve to Helen to the Madonna to Sophia. I am in love with Ayasofya.

I want to treat the place itself as if it were the house that Wisdom built, as in the words "Wisdom has built her house, she has set up her seven pillars."[2] It has the signs of a church, such as the mosaic of the Madonna and Child in the apse, and the signs of a mosque, such as the name of Allah and that of

Muhammad and those of the first caliphs inscribed on giant discs in the corners, but by having at once the signs of a church (the mosaics were whitewashed when it became a mosque) and of a mosque (not yet there, of course, when it was a church), it is clearly a museum. The whole world in our times has become a "museum without walls,"[3] André Malraux says, where works of different ages and cultures and religions coexist and are seen together as works of art and architecture. Here is a challenge to the two postulates I have been making: (1) that it is possible to pass over from the standpoint of one's own life to that of another person, and (2) that God, though called by a different name in every standpoint, is nevertheless one and the same. Can I pass over to the standpoint not only of Christians for whom this place is a church but also of Muslims for whom it is a mosque and of moderns for whom it is a museum? Is the God encountered here, though named and conceived differently in Christianity and Islam and secular modernity, nevertheless one and the same?

I have a clue, a thread I can follow. I can trace certain universal movements of the human spirit that are embodied in the very architecture of this place, in its orientation from end to end and in its convergence upon its center. Somehow the essence of Holy Wisdom is enacted in these movements, the essence of knowing what is enough, of knowing God is enough, the essence of knowing what is necessary and what is sufficient for human beings.

"BEFORE ME, IN ME—WERE YOU ALONE"

On going into Ayasofya you are caught up in the orientation from end to end and in the convergence upon the center. I expected my eyes to be drawn first of all to the center, up to the zenith of the great dome enclosing the inner space, but they were drawn instead to the apse and to the mosaic I saw there of the Madonna and Child. It is as if the orientation from end to end, as a movement of the human spirit, comes before the convergence upon the center. According to Dionysius the Areopagite, writing in the years before the building of the church, there are three movements of the human spirit in contempla-

tion—the linear, the spiral, and the circular.[4] The linear movement, I can see, is embodied in the orientation of the church
from end to end, the spiral in its convergence upon its center,
and the circular in its repose and stability at its center under
the dome.

I can see a hint of Holy Wisdom herself in the design of this
place, in the circle and half-circles, the dome and half-domes,
in the intent "to compound the basilican plan with a central
dome,"[5] to combine orientation from end to end, I will say, with
convergence upon a center. The movements that are embodied
in the architecture are actually carried out by people coming in
from outside, moving around inside, and coming to rest here in
recollection of spirit. They were carried out not only by Christians in the church but also by Muslims in the mosque, and they
are carried out even now by tourists in the museum. Somehow
there is still a power in this place, an awesome feeling of serenity. A young Dutchman I met told me he found it difficult to
leave Ayasofya once he had entered. I feel the same thing, a
reluctance to leave, to step outside of the encompassing peace I
have found here. "I wonder if this is an experience of Holy
Wisdom that I am feeling," I have written in my diary, "a peace
that is stabilizing my heart." As you come into Ayasofya, you
come from the outer to an inner world, you come into an inner
space, but more than that, you come into the inner world of the
spirit. As you move about inside, you move in the world of the
spirit, coming at times to some new illumination of mind, at
times to some new inspiration of heart. And as you come to
rest, maybe in the center, maybe somewhere off from center, a
peace begins to encompass you, a peace that makes you reluctant ever again to leave.

Is it possible to live in peace? Is it possible, I mean, to live in
a peace that stabilizes hearts? I find myself asking now like Solomon for "an understanding mind," for "a discerning heart,"
hoping to live in the peace I am finding here, hoping Ayasofya
herself will come with me on my journey from here. Is understanding of mind, is discernment of heart the necessary and
sufficient condition for a peace that can steady human hearts?
"All good things came to me along with her,"[6] it is said in the
Wisdom of Solomon. According to the story of Solomon, God

was very pleased when he asked for understanding and discernment, and gave him not only what he asked but also what he had not asked, riches and honor and length of days. My question is whether asking for a mind that understands, for a heart that discerns, as I am doing, asking really for Holy Wisdom herself, I am asking somehow for "all good things," for all the human heart desires. Can understanding and discernment satisfy the human heart?

There is abundance, I expect, where God is, where Holy Wisdom is, an abundance of "all good things." It is not as though a mind that understands, a heart that discerns is enough by itself. It is rather God who is enough. The trouble is, as I have been saying, I know and I don't know God is enough for me. If I could go from "know and don't know" to "know," then indeed I would have a mind that understands, a heart that discerns. Maybe if I pass over to Christians first of all, for whom this is "the great church"[7] of Holy Wisdom, I will come to perceive the abundance, and then I will know.

Inscribed in bronze over the main door on a sculpture of an open book are words from John's Gospel:

The Lord said,	if any one
I am	enters,
the door of the	he will be saved,
sheep;	and will go in and out
by me	and find pasture.[8]

I shall take these as key words, suggesting the words of the psalm "The Lord is my shepherd" with its theme of abundance, "I shall not want," and of guard and guiding, "I fear no evil," and of wanting to stay, as I do here, "I shall dwell in the house of the Lord for ever."[9] As I enter by this door, the inscribed words seem to say that I am entering really by the door that is Christ, I am entering the fold of Christ, I will be saved, I will go in and out and find pasture. Actually I do feel, every time I come in here, that I am surrounded by peace. If it is the peace of God, as I believe, I am being saved. If it restores my soul, as I feel, I am going in and out and finding pasture.

I can only imagine what it was like here at the celebration of Christian liturgies. I know what those liturgies were meant to be: "That which was from the beginning," as is said in the prologue of John's Epistle, "which we have heard, which we have seen with our eyes, which we have looked upon and touched with our hands, concerning the Word of life."[10] There was to be a hearing, a seeing, a looking upon, a touching of the Word of life which existed from the beginning. The purpose was something like my own in coming here, seeing with my eyes, feeling in my heart. There were two parts to those liturgies, first the Liturgy of the Catechumens, which was a hearing and a seeing, and then the Liturgy of the Faithful, which was a looking upon and a touching. Everything began at this door where I am standing, people gathered here, waiting for the patriarch and the emperor. When all were ready, they entered, streaming in from the west toward the east, moving along the orientation of the church from end to end.

I enter too now, following their path, and I come at once to an experience of seeing, as I had hoped in coming here, seeing with my own eyes the light and the shadows, the walls and the space. I come also to a feeling of presence, as I had also hoped, feeling in my heart the presence of God here. If I do not separate my eyes and my heart, if I do not separate seeing and feeling, that is, my eyes seeing the light of day shining in through the many windows in these walls, filling this vast inner space and dispersing all the shadows, and my heart feeling the inner light, the divine presence within me, giving spiritual enlightenment and moral guidance and religious assurance as I seek it through faith, then I seem to be coming into a light shining in the darkness. I can see how "the light shines in the darkness," as is said in the prologue of John's Gospel, and how "the darkness has not overcome it."[11] In fact, this sentence, "The light shines in the darkness," corresponds to that other, further on in the prologue, "And the Word became flesh and dwelt among us." The light shining down into the inner space here is how the incarnation of the Word is enacted here.

Over the ages the light has dimmed, the number of open windows and lighted lamps has decreased, changing the effect from one of joy to one of serenity to one of sadness. Still, "the darkness has not overcome it." I can still feel the serenity, and I can even recapture the joy as I reenact the Christian liturgy.

Facing toward the southeast, along the orientation of the church, I am facing toward the dawn. Going all the way back to prehistoric times, there have been peoples who face toward the east to pray, toward the rising sun, for whom the great symbol is a cave, it has been said, and there have been peoples also who face toward the west, towards the setting sun, and for them the great symbol is an altar at the crossroads.[12] I am joining here, it is clear, the people who face east to pray. The cave is a vast one, "the great church" itself. The dawn, I can see, again by not separating my eyes and my heart, is the shining of the light in the darkness, the dawn that is spoken of in Luke's Gospel, "when the day shall dawn upon us from on high to give light to those who sit in darkness and in the shadow of death, to guide our feet into the way of peace."[13]

These are the very words that come to mind now as I go from seeing to hearing, from the First Entrance, as it was called in the Christian liturgy, to the reading of the Gospel, for they seem to be words for what I have been doing without words, going into the sunrise. I read them now, sitting in the northwest corner of the church in front of a marble urn, facing toward the sunrise, using a small New Testament I have been carrying in my pocket. "Through the tender mercy of our God," I read, "whereby the dayspring from on high hath visited us," I read in this version, "to give light to them that sit in darkness and in the shadow of death, to guide our feet into the way of peace."[14] As I read the words of mercy, of dawning, of light shining in the darkness, of guiding into the way of peace, I write them down in my diary, and I write, "This is the meaning of Wisdom here!"

I am hearing the words in my heart, as I read them, only in my heart and not also in my ears. If I were really at a Christian liturgy, I would be hearing words sung and proclaimed. As it is, I am going from seeing with my eyes and my heart to hearing only in my heart. There is a silence here, after these many centuries, broken only by the murmuring voices of visitors and their guides. Still, seeing and hearing with my heart, I am seeing and hearing the essential, I am seeing and hearing "That which was from the beginning." Somehow the silence I hear in my ears, the silence that is broken by murmuring voices, is like the light and the shadows, the walls and the space I see with my eyes. It is a silence that has meaning. It is like a muteness, like the silence out of which the old man Zechariah was speaking when he uttered the words I have been quoting about the dawn. He had become mute because he had not believed the words he heard with his ears. He broke the silence when he came to believe the words in his heart. The silence here is like that, a muteness that comes of unbelief, a silence that can be broken only by believing the words in your heart.

Now comes the turning point in my reenactment of the Christian liturgy, when I go from hearing and seeing to looking upon and touching the Word of life. Everything depends on believing the words I am hearing in my heart, the words of mercy, of dawning, of light shining in the darkness, of guiding into the way of peace. If I can believe, if I can take the words to heart, I expect, I can look upon and touch the Word of life. A helpful and consoling thought occurs to me now: wanting to believe is believing, it can be said, wanting to hope is hoping, wanting to love is loving.[15] I have already taken, according to this, the leap of faith I am trying to take. I am already on the other side of the chasm I am attempting to cross. It is at this point in the Christian liturgy that the Catechumens left the church, the doors were closed, and only the Faithful remained. If I really am on the other side of the abyss of faith, as I am hoping, then I am with the Faithful, and I am ready to see the Entrance of the Mysteries, as it was called, the bringing in of bread and wine, with which the Liturgy of the Faithful begins. I have the eyes and heart, if wanting to believe is believing, to see the bread and wine consecrated and shared and consumed as the body and blood of Christ.

Here again, if I were at a Christian liturgy, I would be actually looking upon bread and wine. As it is, I am looking upon light and shadows, walls and space. Still, I know I am standing in a place where the Christian mysteries were celebrated for almost a thousand years. I am looking toward the apse "which would be the part which faces the rising sun," as Procopius writes in his description of Hagia Sophia, "that portion of the building in which they perform the mysteries in the worship of God."[16] I see only the light shining into the empty space. I do

not see the "mysteries" themselves, the bread and wine. If it is
true, nevertheless, that the heart sees the essential, sees "That
which was from the beginning," then standing here, believing
by wanting to believe, hoping by wanting to hope, loving by
wanting to love, I am looking, I can say, upon the Word of life,
laying myself open to the life-giving Word, to the Word that was
spoken in the beginning, "Let there be light!"

It is as if light were the "mystery" for me, like the bread and
wine in the Christian liturgy, my eyes seeing the light of day
and my heart feeling the presence of God. In fact, I am seeing
and feeling something that was seen and felt already when
Hagia Sophia was still new. Seeing the place filled with light,
Procopius writes:

It abounds exceedingly in sunlight and in the reflection of the sun's
rays from the marble. Indeed one might say that its interior is not
illuminated from without by the sun, but that the radiance comes into
being within it, such an abundance of light bathes this shrine.

And feeling the presence, he writes:

And whenever anyone enters this church to pray, he understands at
once that it is not by any human power or skill, but by the influence of
God, that this work has been so finely turned. And so his mind is lifted
up toward God and exalted, feeling that He cannot be far away, but
must especially love to dwell in this place which He has chosen. And
this does not happen only to one who sees the church for the first time,
but the same experience comes to him on each successive occasion, as
though the sight were a new one each time.[17]

As I see it and feel it, letting the words I have taken to heart
interpret it, the presence is one of mercy, of a dawning light, of
a light shining in the darkness, of a peace guiding us into the
way of peace. It is the presence of Holy Wisdom herself.

My communion, therefore, as I come to reenact the sharing
and the consuming of the "mysteries" in the Christian liturgy,
is to touch the Word of life by letting the light touch me, letting
the light bathe me in its radiance. What happens in Hagia
Sophia, "the radiance comes into being within it" and "an abundance of light bathes this shrine," happens to me standing
inside it, and the presence of God here, who "cannot be far
away, but must especially love to dwell here," becomes presence

in me. There is flesh and blood here, my own, penetrated by the presence I feel all around me. It is as if my flesh and blood were being permeated by light, as if light were shining in my darkness, as if the Word were becoming flesh and dwelling within me. There are often words in Scripture about the hardening of the heart. It is by a softening of the heart, I can see, by the heart becoming tender, that the divine presence can make itself felt. In that conjunction of presence and the softening of the heart, I can see the touch of Holy Wisdom herself. A union is being consummated here, a communion with ultimate reality. I am learning how real Holy Wisdom is and how real a union with her can be.[18]

Here is where my reenactment of the Christian liturgy ends. "So after receiving the precious Body and Blood we say a prayer of thanksgiving," an ancient account says, "and then we go out, each one to his own home."[19] As I go out, though, I find myself hoping and praying Holy Wisdom herself will come with me. I carry with me a memory, of seeing with my eyes and feeling in my heart, of light and presence. I am hoping, though, she will actually come with me, not just that the memory will stay alive but that I will continue somehow to see the light and to feel the presence. In coming here I have been responding to her call, as in Proverbs, inviting me into her house of seven pillars, and in going out, I realize now, I am praying, as in the Wisdom of Solomon, asking for her companionship. I am thinking of her as in the prayer there where she is called "thy Holy Spirit."[20] Indeed, I realize, it is by thinking of her in this way, as the "holy Spirit" of God, that I can envision her as a constant companion.

As I go out under the bronze lintel of the main door and look back again at the inscription over the door, I see again the words "and will go in and out," and I take comfort in the thought of going out, that not only going in but also going out is blessed. It is blessed, I mean, if Holy Wisdom herself comes with me. Going out, I am thinking, is like Pentecost, the Spirit that was in Jesus passes into his disciples and they go out into the world. Jesus Christ is the door, according to the inscription, "I am the door," but the house is the seven-pillared house of Wisdom. I go in to Holy Wisdom by the doorway of Christ, and

I go out by the same door, and the "holy Spirit" that was in Jesus passes into me and comes with me as my companion. I can understand the Christian doctrine of the Trinity in these terms: There is God, and there is the Word that becomes flesh in Jesus, and there is the Spirit that passes from Jesus into his followers.[21]

Looking back upon my experience of Holy Wisdom here, an experience of light and of presence, I can see it is not nearly so concrete as the experience Vladimir Solovyov describes in his poem "Three Meetings" where he tells of his three encounters with Holy Wisdom. One occurred in his boyhood, when he was nine, and he saw her too as a child of nine "suffused with golden azure." Another occurred in youth, when he prayed, asking her why she hadn't revealed herself to him since childhood, and he saw her again, surrounded again "with a golden azure," but this time he saw only her face. And then the final one occurred while he was out in the desert of Egypt, when he prayed to see not only her face but the whole of her being:

> What is, what was, and what will always be—
> A single motionless look encompassed everything here . . .
> The seas and rivers showed dark blue beneath me
> As did the distant forest, and the heights of snowy mountains.
> I saw everything, and everything was one thing only—
> A single image of female beauty . . .
> The infinite fit within its dimensions:
> Before me, in me—were you alone.[22]

I can feel the force of what he is saying, especially the force of those last words, "Before me, in me—were you alone."

If I may take my own experience of light and of presence to be one of spirit and of "holy Spirit," I can say those words too, "Before me, in me—were you alone," meaning I am encountering nothing here in this empty place but light and presence, nothing but spirit and "holy Spirit." What I am lacking is Solovyov's iconlike vision of Holy Wisdom. The church of Hagia Sophia was built in the sixth century in the reign of the emperor Justinian, thus before the age of iconoclasm, the eighth and ninth centuries, and before also the reaction to iconoclasm that shaped the religious vision of subsequent centuries. No shape is given to Holy Wisdom here, therefore, but the shape given by the architecture itself, by the circle and half-circles, the dome and half-domes, by the light and the shadows, the walls and the space. Over the centuries the liturgy changed, however, from "a series of full-scale processional movements" at the First Entrance, the reading of the Gospel, the Entrance of the Mysteries, the Communion and the Exit, to "a series of appearances—the emergence of the clergy from the iconostasis for the Entrances and their return through the Holy Door."[23] I can see the change in the mosaics here, dating of course from the centuries after iconoclasm. I can see it especially in the mosaic that draws my eyes to the apse, the image of the Madonna and Child. Here is my icon of Holy Wisdom.

Who or what is Holy Wisdom? Is she the Madonna? Is she the Spirit? Is she the Word? Is she the divine essence? Each one of these answers has been given at some time or another in the course of the centuries.[24] If I go simply by my own experience here in this place dedicated to Holy Wisdom, I have to find her in an experience of light and of presence. Interpreting my experience, I will say her image is the Madonna, her spirit is the Spirit, her expression is the Word, her essence is the divine essence.

Wisdom is a name of God, as Procopius says simply, telling how the people of this city came to give their church its name Sophia, "an epithet which they have most appropriately invented for God, by which they call His temple" (" 'Sophia' the temple is called by the men of Byzantium," he says in another place, "who consider that this designation is especially appropriate to God").[25] Wisdom is divine, that is to say, God alone is wise, we are only lovers and seekers of Wisdom. Still, the Wisdom of God has become accessible to us, the Word has become flesh and the Spirit has come to dwell in us—that is what I have been learning here, seeing the light and feeling the presence. As I come in, I reenact the Christian liturgy, seeing with my eyes and feeling in my heart. As I go out, I hope and pray to keep on seeing the light and feeling the presence. It is enough for me, I begin to realize, the light in my eyes, the presence in my heart; it is enough to see and to feel. God is enough. I am on the verge of knowing.

"THE LOVERS OF GOD HAVE NO RELIGION BUT GOD ALONE"

If I say "God is enough for me," I am coming very near the Islamic proclamation of divine unity, "There is no god but God." I don't mean I am moving away from the Christian proclamation of the Trinity. Rather I am saying "There is no god for me but God," or even, though I am not sure I am ready yet for this, "There is nothing for me but God." According to Muslim notions, as I have found in conversations here in Istanbul, instead of the Father and the Son and the Holy Spirit, the Trinity that Christians believe in is thought to be the Father and the Mother and the Son. It is a conception that is mentioned in the Koran itself ("O Jesus son of Mary, didst thou say unto men, 'Take me and my mother as gods, apart from God'?").[26] I can see how the conception arose, as I look in through the door of Ayasofya and see the image of the Madonna and Child in the apse. This is what is visible in Christianity to the eyes of an outsider, the Mother and the Child.

An insight comes if we enter into the feeling being expressed in the image, as in the words addressed to Mary in Luke's Gospel, "Blessed are you among women, and blessed is the fruit of your womb!", a feeling not alien to the Koran, as in the words ascribed to Jesus in the Chapter of Mary, "Peace be upon me, the day I was born, and the day I die, and the day I am raised up alive!"[27] It is not a feeling of "gods, apart from God." Rather it is a feeling of divine abundance. If I am ever really able to say "God is enough for me," it will be when I know the divine abundance, when I know the meaning of "blessed," when I know the meaning of "peace." I can see a movement toward that meaning in the very structure of this place, in its convergence upon its center, as if spiraling in toward the center were a movement from the many to the one, while the opposite, spiraling out from the center, were a movement from the one to the many. I can see the same two tendencies in my life, one of convergence, of "simplification through intensity" or of "simplicity that is also intensity," the other of divergence, of "dispersal."[28] I can see them also in the archetypal story of Solomon, the convergence in his early life, in his quest of wisdom, and the divergence in his later life, in his infatuation with many women and with many gods. Somehow the historic transformation of this place, from a church into a mosque, and the Islamic proclamation of divine unity here, calls me or challenges me to convergence.

It is like the call to prayer you can hear at the different times of the day here in Istanbul, the call that is broadcast from the minarets, *Allâh akbar*, "God is greatest," and *lâ ilâh illa-llâh*, "There is no god but God."[29] Those repeated words, *Allâh akbar*, literally "God is greater," make me think of Anselm's definition of God, "that greater than which nothing can be conceived," and they seem to call me to conceive nothing greater than God, to place God before all else, and those other words, *lâ ilâh illa-llâh*, "There is no god but God," make me think of the one and the many, of the young Solomon's wisdom and the old Solomon's infatuation, and they seem to warn me of what I can become, of "no fool like an old fool," and to call me to what I am meant to be, a lover of Holy Wisdom, a lover of God.

What happens to the figure of Holy Wisdom, though, if I follow the call to prayer, if I pass over to Muslims for whom this place is a mosque? I seem to pass over from the figure to the ground, as it were, from the subject to the substance. I will be like Sirach who says, after praising the figure of Holy Wisdom, "All this is the book of the covenant of the Most High God."[30] For if I pass over to Islam, I am passing over to a standpoint where Wisdom is indeed a name of God but the figure of Wisdom has disappeared, where the substance of Wisdom is thought to be contained in the Book. I can bring myself to pass over, if I love her, only to enter into her ground, to plunge into her substance, and with a promise I will come back to her again, to her as figure, to her as subject.

"God is the Light of the heavens and the earth." These words from the Koran, from the Chapter of Light, are inscribed in a circle around the topmost point inside the dome. I shall take them as passwords for entering Ayasofya as a mosque, for they seem to articulate my experience here of light and of presence:

> God is the Light of the heavens and the earth;
> the likeness of His Light is as a niche

wherein is a lamp
(the lamp in a glass,
the glass as it were a glittering star)
kindled from a Blessed Tree,
an olive that is neither of the East nor of the West
whose oil wellnigh would shine, even if no fire touched it;
Light upon Light;
God guides to His Light whom He will.
And God strikes similitudes for men,
and God has knowledge of everything.[31]

I see here an expression of Holy Wisdom, without however the figure, without the subject, an expression in terms of light and implicitly in terms of presence, for the light is the Light that God is, "Light upon Light." If I stand in the light and in the presence, I believe, I will find the ground of Wisdom and the substance.

I cannot go through the motions of prayer here, according to Muslim ritual,[32] in a standing position alternating with inclinations and prostrations. For now the mosque has become a museum and public prayer is forbidden. I can stand in the light, nevertheless, and pray in my heart. I know the ritual motions are important, from having gone through them once at sunset prayer in a small mosque in Jerusalem. It seems especially important to touch one's head to the ground, as is done in the ritual prostrations. When you touch your head to the ground, I felt, your body tells you "God is greatest" and "there is no god but God." I felt then, as I stood facing south toward Mecca, as I bowed, as I touched my head to the ground, as I sat, in unison with all the others, I was learning to be whole before God, to be in God's presence, body as well as soul.

There is something bodily about what I am doing now too, standing here in the light and praying in my heart. Somehow "the fleshly house of the soul" that my body is corresponds to the house of Wisdom in which I am standing. My standing here, even though it does not alternate with bowing and touching my head to the ground and sitting, is bodily and is a bodily expression of my praying. Or it is, I am thinking, if I wish it to be, if I do not separate the two, standing and praying. In fact, this place is full of people who are standing but not praying, who are touring, who are only standing and looking. I am indistinguishable from them except in the secrecy of my heart. Yet maybe they too are praying, some of them, Christians to whom this place is still a church, Muslims to whom it is still a mosque. They don't know if I am praying any more than I do if they are. Is my standing here a bodily expression of my praying if my prayer is secret? Do body and soul separate when you pray in the secrecy of your heart?

I am coming upon something now, I suspect, that can happen in Christianity, something that has happened in secular modernity, a separation of body and soul. A definition of death! Of course I mean rather a separation of bodily attitude and mental attitude, of bearing and feeling. Let me see if I can bring body and soul together again in my standing and praying. Maybe this is what I am to learn from passing over to Islam. I am uneasy, nevertheless, as I stand here facing south toward Mecca to pray. It is the same uneasiness I feel when I hear the second half of the Muslim profession of faith. After *lâ ilâh illa-llâh*, "There is no god but God," comes *we-Muhammad rasûl Allâh*, "and Muhammad is the apostle of God." I want to pass over to Islam, but I do not want to become a Muslim. I am like Ayasofya, it occurs to me as I am standing here. There is a *mihrab*, a niche in the apse, marking the direction of Mecca, the direction of prayer, and yet Ayasofya continues to point, along the lines of its structure, toward the rising sun. It has been given the more southerly direction of a mosque, and yet it retains the more easterly orientation of a church. I am the same. I pass over to Islam, and yet I remain a Christian. I can feel the conflict, as Muslims themselves must have felt it here, between Islam and Christianity.

I feel the conflict begin to resolve only when I pass from the orientation of Ayasofya to its convergence upon its center, when I look up from where I am standing to the zenith, to the topmost point inside the dome. Then the words from the Koran I see inscribed there seem to come true, "God is the Light of the heavens and the earth." Those are the words, I know, that are supposed to have been recited by Mehmet the Conqueror when he came in here, the day the Turks had taken Constantinople. Somehow they express the wonder of Holy Wisdom, the wonder that has always been experienced in this place from the day it was built to the present. Gazing up into it, as I am doing now, as Mehmet did over five hundred years ago, Procopius says, almost a thousand years before that, "it seems not to rest upon solid masonry, but to cover the space with its golden dome (*sphaira*) suspended from heaven," and he tells of how, gazing up, one's "mind is lifted up toward God and exalted."[33]

I am departing now from the ritual of prayer, as it seems, looking up toward the zenith instead of facing in the direction of Mecca. Yet I have heard that to Muhammad himself every prayer (*salât*) was a new Ascension (*mi'raj*), a reenactment of his fundamental experience, his rising up to God in spirit to receive the word of God.[34] That seems to be the sort of experience into which I am being drawn here and now. I say "the sort of experience," meaning not an ecstasy or rapture or transport equal to that of a prophet but simply a lifting of mind and heart and soul to God. The ecstasy of the mind is a kind of trance in which the contemplation of God makes a person oblivious to all else. I am certainly not in a trance now, nor am I oblivious to all else than God. Yet I do find myself becoming absorbed in the thought of God, and I feel the peace, the convergence of thought that comes with being absorbed, the opposite of the divergence I feel when my thoughts are drawn off in all directions. I do not feel effort, a striving to concentrate, as though I had to apply more energy to thinking, but simply the directing of my thoughts to God. I am directing my thoughts myself, it is true, not finding them powerfully taken in that direction without my willing it, as they would be in a true ecstasy. As the peace of being absorbed in God comes over me, nevertheless, I do feel something above and beyond my own desiring and imagining and willing and creating. I feel caught up in something I want to call "Light."

An illumining of the mind, a kindling of the heart, that is how I tend to interpret those words, "God is the Light of the heavens and the earth." What I actually feel is simply a lifting of my mind and heart to God—a classical definition of prayer. A convergence is taking place, though, I can see as I reflect on it, a convergence not only of mind, a process of recollection and composure, but a convergence also of heart, a turning from the many to the one. I feel in me very strongly the centripetal movement, the convergence upon the center, but I cannot help feeling at the same time the shadow at least of its opposite, the centrifugal movement from the one to the many. I feel the love of Wisdom, the longing to live my days in quiet joy, to let my life be shaped by all I have learned on the pilgrimage of my years, that things are meant, there are signs, the heart speaks, there is a way. But I cannot help feeling also an unrequited longing for human love, a kind of wanderlust, a desire to venture onto the unknown paths I have not taken on my life's journey.

It is a choice, then, to go with the converging movement, to go from the many to the one. Convergence is a process like the flowers of an inflorescence developing and expanding successively upward and inward toward a summit, but for human beings the centripetal process, though always trying to come about, never fully takes place unless it is free and willing. I have to choose, either to go with the convergence or to leave myself open to divergence. I would have thought the choice would be between God and no God, but it is more like a choice between the one God and the many gods. I begin to feel the thrust of the words, "There is no god but God." If I do choose to give myself to convergence upon the center, I may hope to live in "a peace that is stabilizing my heart." I can already feel the peace. Choosing, I hope, will enable me to abide in it. Choice adds something to experience, is itself an experience, lets the experience shape my existence. I can still feel the shadow of divergence, though, the unrequited longing, the wanderlust. If there is peace for me, it will come from a presence of the one not from an absence of the many.

In fact, as I come more and more into touch with the divergence I feel, with the unrequited longing, with the wanderlust, I find myself getting caught up in a maelstrom where the centripetal and the centrifugal seem equal and opposite forces. I am getting caught up in the darkness of my soul. Here again the words speak to me, "God is the Light of the heavens and the earth." My choice to go with the convergence upon the center is a choice to let the light I experience here shine in the darkness of my soul. It is a light in which I can see the infatuation that awaits me if I go the way of divergence, going "after strange gods," as it were, like Solomon in his later years. I can see infatuation in the unrequited longing that leads me from person to person, in the wanderlust that leads me from path to path, in my indefinite longing for someone or something I do not have. Somehow the many gods go with the many persons and the many paths, as if the gods were at the far ends of the many radii that converge upon the one center where God is. Yet what am I to do with my longing for human love, with my desire to venture upon unknown paths?

An answer comes to me as I recall again the words of my friend, of being among the giant redwood trees, "The fatigue of the days dropped from us and we were small creatures again in a big world made by God." I am having a very similar experience here, standing in the great encompassing space of Ayasofya. My unrequited longing, my wanderlust is dropping from me, I realize now, with "the fatigue of the days," with the striving to encompass everything myself. I see now I have been striving to encompass everything, going from person to person, from path to path. All this has been dropping from me ever since I set foot in here, but I have been holding on to it, keeping it in mind, wondering what I am to do about it. Now I can let it go, knowing it is only striving and not the heart's desiring. I know it in the light I am seeing, in the presence I am feeling. It is a striving to be all in all. It drops from me like fatigue, the fatigue of all my years, and I am a small creature again in a big world made by God.

I find myself walking around in circles now, around the center beneath the dome, turning slowly as I walk, slowly so as not to draw attention, yet not unlike the whirling dervishes at Konya, slowly whirling in their dance before God. I have been shown the way they whirl with their right hand extended upward to heaven and their left pointing down to earth. "There was a pillar in his house," it is said of Rumi their founder, "and when he was drowned in the ocean of love he used to take hold of that pillar and set himself turning round it."[35] This circling and turning is the bodily movement that goes for me, at this moment, with the converging of mind and heart and soul upon God. I feel, as I circle and turn, a kind of wholeness, as if I

were learning what it is to love "with all your heart, and with all your soul, and with all your mind, and with all your strength."[36]
I am not holding one hand up toward heaven and the other down toward earth, like the dervishes, and yet I can see and feel the link between heaven and earth that seems to be established as I circle and turn around the center below while looking up toward the center above. It is as if the whole dome were revolving as I revolve, above around the zenith, below around the nadir, as if there were a pillar, as in Rumi's house, connecting heaven and earth, and I set myself turning round it. Something important is happening for me; I am linking my mind and my body as I link heaven and earth; I am finding the axis that passes from mind through heart and soul to body as I revolve around the axis that passes from heaven to earth. The link is heart and soul, and when I am heart and soul in prayer, I see now and I feel, then my mind and my body are connected. It is happening for me here, even though I am praying in the secrecy of my heart and soul, even though the movement I am performing with my body could seem, to the eye of an observer, simply that of a tourist surveying the place, slowly rotating the angle of view.

I see and feel now, as I give myself to the converging of mind and heart and soul upon God, the point of the words Dag Hammarskjold uses to sum up Rumi, "The lovers of God have no religion but God alone."[37] To say "no religion but God alone" is like saying "no god but God." I am passing over from Christianity to Islam, from one religion to another, and yet I remain a Christian, just as Ayasofya, while a mosque, remains still a church in its orientation. I am being caught up, nevertheless, in a converging upon a center, caught up bodily in a converging upon God that contrasts with a diverging toward the gods. It is not the orientation of a religion that contrasts with the worship of the gods, I can see, especially not the bodily enactment of the orientation, facing the sunrise or the sunset, facing a sacred place, as Mecca or Jerusalem. It is rather the converging that contrasts with the diverging, "Purity of heart is to will one thing" with "The will is falling asunder."[38]

When you are caught up in the diverging, "The will is falling asunder," as Yeats says, "but without explosion and noise." There is a quiet disintegration going on, a separation of mind and heart, of heart and soul, of soul and body. "The separated fragments," he says, "seek images rather than ideas." Thus the many gods, corresponding to the many images and the many fragments of will. When you are caught up rather in the converging, as I am now, you find yourself becoming more and more single-minded, single-hearted, single-souled, coming, as Kierkegaard says, "to will one thing." The separated fragments of your will, the many images of paths and persons, begin to lose their independent existence in your sight and in your feeling. Something is happening to your sight and to your feeling, an iconoclasm, a shattering of images, or then again a quiet integration "without explosion and noise," a coming to insight into the images that ends in "no religion but God alone." I think of the very process I am engaged in here, trying to come to insight into the images of my life and the fragments of my will, hoping to find the focus of my seeing and my feeling.

It is one thing, I realize, to see the focus, the point at which all the lines of a life converge and from which they diverge, and it is another to be at the focus and see everything else from there. It is one thing, that is, to go with the converging movement of love, to "have no religion but God alone," and it is another to enter into "the union of love with God," to see with God's eyes and to feel with God's heart. I come here to the farthest pole of Islam. If I go all the way to the center, I find myself in the place Al-Hallaj was standing when he uttered the words for which he was condemned to death, "The Truth has entered me, I am the Truth, no longer I myself."[39]

There is a danger here, I can see, of losing my sense of being a small creature in a big world made by God and of striving again to encompass everything myself. I find here, nevertheless, a glimpse of what I have been seeking, the standpoint of Holy Wisdom, of seeing with God's eyes and feeling with God's heart. It is the standpoint out of which Jesus is speaking in John's Gospel, it seems, when he says "I am," when he too says "I am the Truth."[40] I have to be careful, though, to differentiate myself from what I am seeing and feeling, to say to myself, as I did before, "God dwells in you" rather than "God dwells in you as you." As I move into the center of Ayasofya, acting out bodily the thought in my mind, I find myself looking along the lines radiating out from the center. I begin to see and to feel differently, as if with God's eyes and heart, as if to walk those paths out from the center were to walk with God rather than to go "after strange gods." I think again of the young Turkish woman who told me I was in love with Ayasofya. "Turn to life," she said, "God is in your heart!"

"I CANNOT DISPENSE WITH SOMETHING GREATER THAN MYSELF"

I am at a turning point now. Once I am in the center there is nowhere to go except away from the center. Either I stay in the center or I go out toward the circumference, I "turn to life." A well-known image comes back to mind: God is an infinite sphere whose center is everywhere and whose circumference is nowhere. Once I have found the center, I could say, varying the image, the center goes with me wherever I go, "God is in your heart." I fear to leave the fixed center, though, I fear I will be going from one to the many, from "simplicity that is also intensity" to mere "dispersal." I know I will be entering into the movement that gives rise to secular modernity, into "the metamorphosis of the gods," that occurred in the Renaissance in Europe. A figure from the time of the Renaissance gives me hope, Nicolas of Cusa, who came to the central insight of his life on his way back from Constantinople to Venice. He uses the very image I am contemplating, that of a God whose center is everywhere and whose circumference is nowhere. For Cusa it meant seeing, a few years even before Copernicus, that earth cannot be the fixed center of the universe, "that this earth really moves though to us it seems stationary."[41] For me it means seeing that God is not an Archimedean point where I can stand outside the world, that I can find God in my heart only by turning somehow to life.

How though? Cusa speaks of "a learned ignorance," a knowing by way of unknowing. There is a blind spot in my seeing and in my feeling, like "the blind spot," as it is called, in the retina of the eye, the point in the retina not sensitive to light. Seeing with God's eyes and feeling with God's heart would mean seeing where I am now blind and feeling where I am now insensitive. It would mean turning to life indeed but taking into account the blindness there is in my seeing of life, the insensitivity there is in my feeling for life. By taking into account my own blindness and insensitivity I will be practicing "learned ignorance," knowing by way of my unknowing.

If I forget about the blind spot and think of myself nevertheless as being always in the focus of seeing and of feeling, then the center is still everywhere, but it is the center simply of the universe, not God that is everywhere. That is the history of this metaphor of the infinite sphere. First it was an image of God, but then it became an image simply of the universe.[42] Its history is that of secular modernity. If I am to pass over into secular modernity without losing everything I have gained in passing over into Christianity and into Islam, then I have to let the empty center become full of presence, I have to "practice the presence of God."[43] Seeing and feeling are a matter of perception; presence is a matter of awareness. If I become aware of the unseeing in my seeing, of the unfeeling in my feeling, I come by way of awareness to what is beyond my perception. My awareness of unseeing becomes a seeing; my awareness of unfeeling becomes a feeling. I have God's eyes and heart.

My blind spot, it seems, is in my seeing of life, my insensitivity is in my feeling for life—thus the words that spoke to me, "Turn to life, God is in your heart!" I have something to learn by passing over into secular modernity, something I know and don't know, something to do with God, as Van Gogh said, being more than the God of Falstaff, more than "the inside of a church."[44] I know, I know "God is in your heart," and yet I don't know, I have to "turn to life." I have found Ayasofya in "the inside of a church," but now, as I prepare to leave, I hope to come to an insight, like Cusa on his return voyage, I hope and pray Ayasofya herself will come with me.

"I was returning by sea from Greece" (that is, from Constantinople), Cusa says, "when, by what I believe was a supreme gift of the Father of Lights from Whom is every perfect gift, I was led in the learning that is ignorance to grasp the incomprehensible."[45] He came, that is, to know God. "And this I was able to achieve," he says, "not by way of comprehension but by tran-

scending those perennial truths that can be reached by reason."
He came to know God, that is, not by way of undoubted and
self-evident truths but by way of truths and opposing truths, by
way of "a coincidence of opposites." These are the two essential
parts of his insight, "a learned ignorance" (*docta ignorantia*) and
"a coincidence of opposites" (*coincidentia oppositorum*), as if the
light of God to us were darkness and the presence of God to
us were absence. I shall take these as watchwords, "a learned
ignorance" and "a coincidence of opposites," as I try to come
to a similar insight by entering into the darkness that is my own
unseeing, by entering into the absence that is my own unfeeling.

I wonder if the insight is connected somehow with leaving
Constantinople, as Cusa did and as I am preparing to do, with
leaving Hagia Sophia as "the inside of a church." No doubt, if
you came here to see "the inside of a church," you are disap-
pointed. I think of Mark Twain's reaction:

I do not think much of the Mosque of St. Sophia. I suppose I lack
appreciation. We will let it go at that. It is the rustiest old barn in
heathendom. I believe all the interest that attaches to it comes from
the fact that it was built for a Christian church and then turned into a
mosque, without much alteration, by the Mohammendan conquerors of
the land. They made me take off my boots and walk into the place in
my stocking-feet. I caught cold, and got myself so stuck up with a
complication of gums, slime, and general corruption, that I wore out
more than two thousand pair of boot-jacks getting my boots off that
night, and even then some Christian hide peeled off with them. I abate
not a single boot-jack.[46]

It is as if Falstaff had carried out his threat and actually gone
to see "the inside of a church":

Well, I'll repent, and that suddenly, while I am in some liking. I shall
be out of heart shortly, and then I shall have no strength to repent.
And I have not forgotten what the inside of a church is made of, I am
a peppercorn, a brewer's horse. The inside of a church! Company,
villainous company, hath been the spoil of me.[47]

If I were Falstaff, if I were Mark Twain, if I had come here to
see "the inside of a church," I wouldn't be reluctant to leave. I
should be anxious to get out of here, to get free of this encompassing space. As it is, I am coming out of an encompassing

peace and going out into the wide open space of the universe. Is God the inside of a soul? Is God the inside of a universe?

Here I come upon "a learned ignorance" and "a coincidence of opposites." I know God and I don't know; God is and is not the inside of a church, of a soul, of a universe. There is a relation between outside and inside. As in all architecture, according to Le Corbusier, "the exterior results from the interior."[48] It is especially true of Ayasofya, for the exterior, before you go in, is a "bewildering mountain"[49] of dome and half-domes and buttresses and minarets. The meaning of the whole becomes clear only when you go inside and enter into the orientation from end to end and the convergence upon the center. When you come out again, however, as I am doing now, you are going from convergence to divergence, away from the center, you are reversing the orientation, going now from east to west. It is as if I were going now with the peoples who pray facing toward the sunset rather than the sunrise, whose symbol is an altar at the crossroads rather than a cave. "And only when the pure sky again looks through broken ceilings and down upon grass and red poppies near broken walls," Nietzsche's Zarathustra says, "will I again turn my heart to the abodes of this God,"[50] only when they cease to be caves, that is, and become altars at the crossroads.

Or, more likely and less fanciful, only when they have tumbled down and fallen into decay, he is saying, "will I again turn my heart to the abodes of this God," only when they cease to be churches and become ruins, objects of regret and nostalgia. In a way that is what has actually happened here, Ayasofya has ceased to be a church, ceased to be a mosque, and become a museum. My leaving the place now is my physical act of passing over to secular modernity. As I leave Ayasofya as *it*, hoping and praying Ayasofya as *she* will come with me, as I turn to life, believing God is in my heart, the church is ceasing to be the abode of Holy Wisdom for me, the mosque is ceasing to be the abode of God, it is becoming only a museum to me, only a monument of architecture. I am running a risk, nevertheless, as I leave, of losing touch with Holy Wisdom, as I turn to life, like Nietzsche with his "God is dead," of losing God.

I am enacting "a coincidence of opposites," I can see, as I go from inside to outside, from convergence to divergence, from facing sunrise and birth to facing sunset and death. As I do so, I am abolishing for myself all sense of a fixed circumference, a fixed center, a fixed orientation of prayer and I am coming to a sense of a center that is everywhere, a circumference that is nowhere, a God who is everywhere and nowhere. The danger, I can see, is in that word *nowhere*, the danger of losing God. It is the danger that is inherent in secular modernity. As Cusa says, "There will be a *machina mundi* whose center, so to speak, is everywhere, whose circumference is nowhere, for God is its circumference and center and He is everywhere and nowhere."[51] There, at the very moment he is anticipating Copernicus and the modern vision of the universe, Cusa is speaking of a God who is nowhere as well as everywhere. I can't seem to have the truth of "everywhere" without the opposing truth of "nowhere."

Actually for Cusa, as for Anselm, God is "that greater than which nothing can be conceived," only instead of going on to say "truth" or "existence" is that greater thing, he goes on, like Anselm, to say God is greater than anything we can conceive, God is beyond all our conceptions. Thus he comes to "a learned ignorance." If I go with him now, I am saying God is and is not what I am seeing, for I can see the inside of the universe, or all of it that is visible to the naked eye, and I am saying God is and is not what I am feeling, for I can feel the inside of my soul. Still, I would say, it is not by seeing God or feeling God that I know God but by seeing with God's eyes and feeling with God's heart. It is not by perception, in other words, but by awareness that I come to know God.

Here is my answer to "everywhere and nowhere," my interpretation of "a learned ignorance," my resolution of "a coincidence of opposites." God is the dark to perception, the light to awareness; God is absent to perception, present to awareness.[52] Let me begin with the light and the dark, with my seeing and my unseeing. It is life that I am seeing and not seeing, seeing because I am in it already without my choosing, not seeing because I have not turned to it. When you take up painting, for instance, you begin to see colors you never saw before, never saw because you never paid attention to them. That is what it means to "turn to life," I believe—to pay attention. Before I

came here, before I entered into the hearing and seeing and
looking upon and touching I found here in Christianity, the
bringing of body and soul together I found here in Islam, I had
been living in an unawareness, I realize now, living in a separation of soul and body. I have found here a way of letting sense
be pervaded by spirit, of letting body become in truth "the
fleshy house of the soul."

Now, as I turn to life, I begin to see what I have not been
seeing. "I want to paint men and women with that something of
the eternal which the halo used to symbolize," Van Gogh says,
"and which we seek to convey by the actual radiance and vibra-
tion of our coloring."[53] I have learned something of this kind of
seeing by looking at the mosaics here, the images of the Madonna and Child, of the saints and angels, of the emperors and
empresses, but now, as I turn to life, I begin to see in this way
the mother and child, the men and women, "these commonplace
figures,"[54] as Van Gogh calls them, that I meet in everyday life.
I see them as before with my eyes but now I am aware of the
unseen in them, of "that something of the eternal." It is something I have glimpsed before, a flickering light, as it were,
something I have seen especially in the poor and the hungry
and the sorrowful and the outcast, but now it begins to be more
of a steady light, or so I wish it to be, more of a settled awareness.

"In life and in painting I can quite well dispense with God,"
Van Gogh says. "But suffering as I am, I cannot dispense with
something greater than myself, something that is my whole life:
the power of creating."[55] I can dispense with God as a subject
of life and of painting, he is saying, but not as "that something
of the eternal" I can see in others, not as "something greater
than myself" I can feel in myself that enables me to create. As
I consider what he is saying here, being able and unable to
dispense with God, I realize it bears upon what I have been
saying, knowing and not knowing God. I am asking "Is God
sufficient?" He is asking "Is God necessary?" When he speaks
of "the power of creating" here, I think of the process I spoke
of before, imagining what you desire, willing what you imagine,
and creating what you will. When he says "something greater
than myself," though, I am led deeper into my desiring and
imagining and willing and creating to find the God who is

absent to my perception but present to my awareness. I find I am indeed aware of something greater than myself at work in me as I desire and imagine and will and create. I can discern a presence in the contrast of presence and absence, because at times there is an absence when I am unable to create or to will or to imagine or even to desire.

So it is both with seeing and with feeling. At times I am aware, at times I am unaware of "that something of the eternal" in others, of "something greater than myself" at work in me. At times I can see the light, that is, I can feel the presence; at times I can see only the inside of the universe, I can feel only the inside of my soul. "God is sufficient," I think to myself when I can see the eternal in other people, when I can feel the creating power at work in myself. "God is necessary," I think to myself, on the other hand, when I see only "these commonplace figures," when I feel empty of desire and of imagination and of will and of the power to create.

As I go back and forth between awareness and unawareness, between "God is sufficient" and "God is necessary," I am "practicing the presence of God," I am learning what it means to "pray without ceasing."[56] Or so I think now. It is true, having read Brother Lawrence on the presence of God and the Russian pilgrim on unceasing prayer, I had expected to attain a simple and unchanging awareness of light and of presence. What I have actually found is something more like day and night, an awareness of the light and of the dark, an awareness of presence and of absence, an awareness of awareness and of unawareness. It is truly "a learned ignorance" and "a coincidence of opposites," a knowing of knowing and of unknowing. There is something steady and settled, nevertheless, about the awareness that encompasses the opposing states of awareness and unawareness. It is a steady light even in the dark, a steady presence even in the absence. It is, as I had hoped, *a peace that stabilizes hearts*. I am holding on to God, it seems, while I swing between sufficiency and necessity.

Is it God, though, who is necessary and sufficient? Is "something greater than myself" the same as "that greater than which nothing can be conceived"? I think so, because of this very thing I am discovering, "a peace that stabilizes hearts." Here is my argument. Where peace is, there is God, I want to say, and where God is, there is peace. If I find it on "the inside of a church," on the inside of a mosque, I find it also when I turn to life, dwelling in my heart. It is "the peace of God, which passes all understanding."[57] So it can subsist, I find, in knowing and in unknowing, in light and in darkness, in presence and in absence.

To say this, to say the peace of God subsists not only in the day but also in the night of the soul, "in knowing and in unknowing, in light and in darkness, in presence and in absence," sounds like a marriage vow "for better, for worse; for richer, for poorer; in sickness and in health." Maybe to speak in this way is indeed to make a vow rather than to make a simple statement of fact. Maybe union with God is enacted by vow, is a covenant with God. Or maybe it can be a covenant with Holy Wisdom, like the covenant Ruth made with Naomi, "Entreat me not to leave you or to return from following you; for where you go I will go, and where you lodge I will lodge."[58] These are the words I desire to say now to Ayasofya, leaving the place where she lodges, hoping she will come with me, and also the words that follow, "your people shall be my people, and your God my God," considering my journey with her a journey like that of the Israelites, a journey with God. What I am doing, if I make such a vow, if I enter into such a covenant, is resolving all loneliness and regret, settling with whatever can deter me from the love of Wisdom, from "to have and to hold," from "to love and to cherish," the loneliness and the regret that are felt in the night rather than in the day of the soul.

"We have our loneliness and our regret with which to build an eschatology,"[59] Peter Porter says in a poem, speaking of secular modernity. Our loneliness, I think, is our sense of God's absence, our unfulfilled longing for God that runs unseeing through all our relations with one another, making human relations take all the weight of expectation that only a relation with God can bear. Our regret is our sense of the darkness of the human heart, our longing for a kindling of heart that runs unfeeling through all our feelings, making commonplace feelings take on a role in our lives that only the infinite passion of a faith can sustain. An eschatology is a sense of human purpose or human destiny, but built out of our loneliness and our regret it is unseeing and unfeeling.

If I resolve my loneliness, I am not ridding myself of loneliness so much as coming to understand it, to see what I have not been seeing, or more accurately, to be aware of my unseeing, of the blind spot in my relations with other human beings where I have been expecting them to fulfill a longing only God can fulfill. I am coming to "a learned ignorance" in the matters of the heart, a knowing of my heart's unknowing. I can discern between Holy Wisdom and my own heart, for though I come to an insight into my heart's longing, my heart continues to long for intimacy, to long for understanding, and to look indiscriminately to God and to other human beings. If I were passing over into pagan antiquity, I would say I was entering into a relation with Holy Wisdom like that of Odysseus the fabulous voyager with Athene the goddess of wisdom, a relation of guard and of guiding that leaves room for human intimacy with human beings. And so I am. Yet there is more to it than that, just because this is the Wisdom of God and not the goddess of wisdom. There is something here that touches upon our deep heart's longing and so touches upon all human intimacies and upon all relationships with human beings.

If I resolve my regret, accordingly, the disappointment, the sense of lost opportunity, the heartache arising from the human intimacies, the human relations of my life, I am letting Holy Wisdom touch my heart and heal my memories, kindle my heart and illumine my mind; I am letting her meet pain of mind and spiritual anguish with "a peace that stabilizes hearts." Loneliness is the feeling of being alone combined with the longing to be unalone; regret is the feeling of paradise lost, of happiness lost, of innocence lost. They come together in a nostalgia, a yearning for union and reunion, at bottom, I think, for union and reunion with God. I am coming here, it seems, to "a coincidence of opposites" in the matters of the heart, an intimacy in distance, a distance in intimacy, the intimacy of having Holy Wisdom herself to guard and guide me on all my journeys, the distance of still feeling all my longing and my yearning.

"It is hard to leave this place," I have written in my diary, "but Wisdom will go with me." As I do finally leave and begin

my travels with Holy Wisdom, as I think of Odysseus and his
many voyages with Athene the goddess of wisdom to guard and
guide him, as I think of his longing and his yearning, I wonder
if I am falling into a story like his,

> this song of the various-minded man
> who after he had plundered
> the innermost citadel of hallowed Troy
> was made to stray grievously
> about the coasts of men
> the sport of their customs good or bad
> while his heart
> through all the sea-faring
> ached in an agony to redeem himself
> and bring his company safe home.[60]

It is Lawrence of Arabia, ironically enough, who translates here
the prologue to *The Odyssey*, Lawrence whose life is an almost
literal enactment of these words. I think, as I read them, of the
story as a metaphor, of passing over and coming back, of the
passing over I have been doing here, to Christianity, to Islam,
to secular modernity, and of the coming back I have to do now,
to my own life and times. Perhaps the coming back is the real
odyssey for me too, where I need Holy Wisdom most of all for
my companion and my guide.

NOTES

1. Kings 3:9 and 9:3.
2. Proverbs 9:1.
3. André Malraux, *The Metamorphosis of the Gods* (Garden City, N.Y.: Doubleday, 1960), p. 22.
4. Dionysius, *The Divine Names*, Chapter 4, in *Dionysius the Areopagite*, trans. C. E. Rolt (New York: Macmillan, 1940), pp. 98–99. Cf. Aquinas, *Summa Theologiae*, II–II, q. 180, a. 6 (this is where I first came across the idea).
5. Heinz Kähler, *Hagia Sophia*, trans. Ellyn Childs (New York & Washington: Praeger, 1967), p. 14.
6. Wisdom of Solomon 7:11.
7. Procopius of Caesarea, *Buildings* (Book I, Chapter 1, line 66), trans. H. B. Dewing (London: Heinemann, 1954), p. 29.
8. John 10:7 and 9. Cf. Kähler, *Hagia Sophia*, p. 30 and illustration 62.
9. Psalm 23:1 and 4 and 6.
10. 1 John 1:1. For an ancient account of the liturgy, cf. *The Mystagogia* of St. Maximus the Confessor, trans. Julian Stead, *The Church, the Liturgy*

and the Soul of Man (Still River, Mass.: St. Bede's, 1982). For a modern account, cf. Thomas F. Mathews, *The Early Churches of Contantinople* (University Park and London: Pennsylvania State University Press, 1971), pp. 138–143.

11. John 1:5 and 14.
12. Cf. W. B. Yeats, *A Vision* (New York: Macmillan, 1961), pp. 258f. (and note on p. 259 and also note on p. 204) (Yeats is quoting here the work of the German traveler Frobenius.).
13. Luke 1:78–79.
14. Here I am quoting the King James Version of the same passage.
15. I was going to ascribe this thought to St. Francis de Sales, but I find, on rereading the passage I had in mind, he says only you can believe and hope and love without being aware of it:

> This is exactly what happens when a man is weighed down by inner trials. Though he is quite capable of believing in, hoping in, and loving God; though he actually does so—yet he is too weak to be aware of it. So powerfully does his distress engross and overwhelm him, he cannot come to himself, to see what he is about. For this reason he imagines he has neither faith, hope, nor charity, but only shadows, useless impressions of these virtues, which he feels almost without being aware of them, which seem foreign, not familiar to his soul.

> St. Francis de Sales, *The Love of God* (Book IX, Chapter 12), trans. Vincent Kerns (London: Burns & Oates, 1962), p. 385.

16. Procopius, *Buildings* (Book I, Chapter 1, line 31), p. 17.
17. Ibid. (lines 29–31 and 61–63), p. 17 and p. 27.
18. I think of a remark of Marie Louise von Franz (after quoting Jung saying "I only know now how real these things are"): "Might it not be that St. Thomas Aquinas too, only experienced on his deathbed, when the Song of Songs flooded back into his memory, how real Wisdom and a union with her can be?", in her preface to *Aurora Consurgens*, trans. R. F. C. Hull and A. S. B. Glover (New York: Random House—Pantheon, 1966), p. xiii.
19. The patriarch Eutychius as quoted by Mathews in *The Early Churches of Constantinople*, p. 173.
20. Cf. Proverbs 1:20–21, 8:1–3, 9:3 on the call of Wisdom. Cf. Wisdom of Solomon 9 for the prayer, especially 9:17 ("thy holy Spirit"). Cf. also Wisdom of Solomon 7:22–25 for a description of her as spirit.
21. Here I am going to side with St. Irenaeus, taking Holy Wisdom to be the Holy Spirit. Cf. St. Irenaeus, *Against the Heresies*, Book IV, Chapter 20, in *The Ante-Nicene Fathers*, ed. Alexander Roberts and James Donaldson (New York: Christian Literature Company, 1896), pp. 487–488 ("For with Him were always present the Word and Wisdom, the Son and the Spirit, by whom and in whom, freely and spontaneously, He made all things . . . ") and p. 488 ("I have also largely demonstrated, that the Word, namely the Son, was always with the Father; and that Wisdom also, which is the Spirit, was present with Him, anterior to all creation, He declares by Solomon: 'God by Wisdom founded the earth . . . ' ").
22. Vladimir Solovyov, "Three Meetings," trans. Ralph Koprince, in Carl and Ellendea Proffer (eds.), *The Silver Age of Russian Culture* (Ann Arbor, Mich.: Ardis, 1975), p. 132. Cf. Sergius Bulgakov, *The Wisdom of God* (New York: Paisley, 1937), pp. 23ff. on Solovyov. Cf. also the Russian

icon of Sophia (showing her distinct from the Madonna, with Christ behind her, John the Baptist to her right, and the Madonna to her left) in Paul Evdokimov, *L'art de l'icone* (Paris: Desclee de Brouwer, 1970), p. 295.

23. Mathews, *The Early Churches of Constantinople*, p. 178.

24. On the Madonna cf. Ilene H. Forsyth, *The Throme of Wisdom* (Princeton, N.J.: Princeton University Press, 1972) on wood sculptures of the Madonna in Romanesque France where she is shown holding the Child on her lap and is seen as the "seat of Wisdom" (*sedes sapientiae*). On the Spirit as Wisdom cf. St. Irenaeus cited above in note 21. On the Word as Wisdom cf. St. Athanasius arguing with the Arians who put together the words "Christ the power of God and the wisdom of God" (1 Corinthians 1:24) and the words of Wisdom "The Lord created me at the beginning of his work" (Proverbs 8:22), in *Select Treatises of St. Athanasius*, trans. John Henry Newman (London: Longmans, 1903), 1:272–342, and also Newman's note on Wisdom, 2:334–336. On the divine essence as Wisdom cf. St. Augustine saying "the Father is wisdom, the Son is wisdom, the Holy Spirit is wisdom" in his treatise on *The Trinity*, trans. Stephen McKenna (Washington, D.C.: Catholic University of America Press, 1963), p. 229, and that the Son (the Word) can be called "born Wisdom" (*nata sapientia*) (the translator here says "begotten wisdom," p. 224). St. Thomas Aquinas adopts this view in his *Summa Contra Gentiles*, Book IV, Chapter 12 (where he uses the term *sapientia concepta*), Sergius Bulgakov, speaking for modern Russian "sophiology," says Wisdom is the divine essence (*ousia*) but wants to insist that the divine essence is not something impersonal and is embodied in the personal figures of Wisdom and of Glory, indeed that "Ousia = Sophia = Glory" in his book, *The Wisdom of God*, p. 56.

25. Procopius, *Buildings* (Book I, Chapter 1, line 21), p. 11, and *History of the Wars* (Book III, Chapter 6, line 26), trans. H. B. Dewing, in *Procopius*, vol. 2 (London: Heinemann, 1916), p. 63. It is strange in this second place that he calls the church also "the sanctuary of Christ the Great God," a pagan-sounding title, even though the name of Christ is used, almost like "Great is Artemis of the Ephesians!" (Acts 19:28 and 34).

26. Koran 5:116, trans. Arthur J. Arberry, *The Koran Interpreted* (New York: Macmillan, 1955), 1:147. Cf. Geoffrey Parrinder, *Jesus in the Qu'ran* (London: Faber & Faber, 1965), pp. 133–137.

27. Luke 1:42 and Koran 19:34 (Arberry, *The Koran Interpreted*, vol. 1, p. 333). Cf. Parrinder, *Jesus in the Qu'ran*, p. 28.

28. W. B. Yeats, *A Vision* (New York: Collier, 1966), pp. 140–141.

29. Cf. "The Call to Prayer," trans. De Lacy O'Leary, in his *Colloquial Arabic* (London: Kegan Paul and New York: Dutton, 1950), p. 177.

30. Sirach (Ecclesiasticus) 24:23. Cf. also Baruch 4:1.

31. Koran 24:35 (Arberry, *The Koran Interpreted*, vol. 2, pp. 50–51.

32. For a detailed description of Muslim ritual cf. Edwin Elliott Calverley, *Worship in Islam* (Cairo: American University, School of Oriental Studies, 1957), pp.3–34.

33. Procopius, *Buildings* (Book I, Chapter 1, line 46), p. 21, and (line 61), p. 27.

34. Cf. Reynold A. Nicholson, *Rumi* (London: Allen & Unwin, 1950), p. 92. Cf. my book, *The Way of All the Earth* (New York: Macmillan, 1972), p. 112 for a discussion of Muhammad's experience.

35. Cf. A. J. Arberry, *The Rubaiyat of Jalal al-Din Rumi* (London: Emery Walker, 1949), p. xxiii.
36. Mark 12:30. Cf. also Luke 10:27 and Matthew 22:37, going back to Deuteronomy 6:5.
37. Dag Hammarskjold, *Markings*, trans. Leif Sjöberg and W. H. Auden (New York: Knopf, 1964), p. 103.
38. *Purity of Heart Is to Will One Thing* is the title of a work by Sören Kierkegaard, trans. Douglas V. Steere (New York: Harper & Row, 1965). "The will is falling asunder" is an expression of W. B. Yeats in *A Vision*, p. 141. Cf. the comparison of the two ideas in my book, *The Church of the Poor Devil* (New York: Macmillan, 1982), p. 30.
39. Herbert Mason, *The Death of Al-Hallaj* (Notre Dame, Ind. and London: University of Notre Dame Press, 1979), p. 54.
40. John 14:6.
41. Nicolas Cusanus, *Of Learned Ignorance*, trans. Germain Heron (London: Routledge & Kegan Paul, 1954), p. 111.
42. Cf. Jorge Luis Borges, *Other Inquisitions*, trans. Ruth L. C. Simms (New York: Washington Square Press, 1966), pp. 5–8. Cf. also my discussion and use of the metaphor in the last paragraph of my book, *The Way of All the Earth*, p. 232.
43. Brother Lawrence (Nicolas Herman), *The Practice of the Presence of God* (Mt. Vernon, N.Y.: Peter Pauper Press, 1963).
44. Cf. Vincent Van Gogh, letter to Theo of July 1880 (letter #133) in W. H. Auden, *Van Gogh: A Self-Portrait* (Greenwich, Conn.: New York Graphic Society, 1961), p. 53.
45. Nicolas Cusanus, *Of Learned Ignorance*, p. 173.
46. Mark Twain (Samuel Langhorne Clemens), *The Innocents Abroad* (Hartford, Conn.: American Publishing Co., 1869), p. 362.
47. Shakespeare, *1 Henry IV*, act 3, sc. 2, lines 8–9.
48. Le Corbusier (Edouard Jeanneret-Gris), *Towards a New Architecture*, trans. Frederick Etchells (New York: Payson & Clark, 1927), p. 183.
49. Kähler, *Hagia Sophia*, p. 22.
50. Friedrich Wilhelm Nietzsche, *Thus Spake Zarathustra*, trans. Walter Kaufmann, in *The Portable Nietzsche* (New York: Viking, 1954), pp. 203–204.
51. Nicolas Cusanus, *Of Learned Ignorance*, p. 111.
52. Here I am using a distinction Bernard Lonergan makes between "perception" (*conscientia-perceptio*) and "experience" (*conscientia-experientia*) (I am using the term *awareness*) in his discussion of the consciousness of Christ, "Christ as Subject: A Reply," in *Collection* (New York: Herder & Herder, 1967), pp. 175–192. His point is that the basic self-awareness of Christ is not a perception of himself as an object but an awareness of himself as a subject.
53. Van Gogh, letter to Theo of September 3, 1888 (letter #531) in Auden, *Van Gogh*, p. 319.
54. Van Gogh, letter to Theo in July 1883 (letter #418), in Auden, *Van Gogh*, p. 243.
55. This is also from letter #531, but here I am quoting it from the epigraph of Malraux's book, *The Metamorphosis of the Gods*, as translated by Stuart Gilbert, the place where I first saw it.
56. 1 Thessalonians 4:17 (King James Version). Cf. *The Way of a Pilgrim* by an anonymous Russian pilgrim, trans. R. M. French (New York: Harper, 1952).

57. Philippians 4:7.
58. Ruth 1:16.
59. As quoted by Frank Kermode in *The Sense of an Ending* (London: Oxford University Press, 1981), p. 2.
60. T. E. Lawrence, *The Odyssey of Homer* (New York: Oxford University Press, 1932), page before p. 1.

3. "Things are meant"

on starting on
a wanderyear of soul

A light, a presence—that is what I have found on my pilgrimage to the house of Wisdom, a peace you can find also in nature,
in the Grand Canyon, for instance, or among the giant redwood
trees, something you cannot find, as it seems, in human affairs.
Still, I wonder, as I return now to human affairs, to my life and
my times, if you cannot find Wisdom at work here too, if you
cannot find a hidden presence here, a meaning in unmeaning
things of life.

If I say "Things are meant," as I have been doing until now,
I am speaking out of a way of taking the things of life, taking
them as things that happen on a journey with God in time. I
have been taking the things of my life as belonging to my life,
the meeting of friends, for instance, and their parting, taking
also the things of my times as belonging to my times, the rise
of peoples, for instance, and their decline and fall, taking them
all as incidents belonging to a story. Now I want to find if I am
doing something more than making a story of my life and times,
if there really is a presence, though it be hidden, if there really
is a meaning, though things seem unmeaning apart from the
story I tell, to find if I am discovering, that is, and not just
inventing. I am starting on a wanderyear of soul, a new story I
can tell of feeling and of seeing, to feel if I can feel a presence,
to see if I can see a meaning.

A wanderyear is a year of travel before settling down to your
occupation in life. A wanderyear of soul, as I am envisioning it,
is a period of soul-searching before choosing your way in life
and in time. I am always choosing my way, I realize, and have
been choosing all along, but now I have to choose with a new
awareness of God and of the Wisdom of God. I am on dangerous ground, saying "Things are meant." I am in danger of

falling into an illusion of "historical inevitability," thinking there is no real choosing, of falling prey to notions "which tend to make us accept whatever happens as irresistible and foolhardy to oppose."[1] On the other hand, there is an equal and opposite danger of giving up the quest "to make sense of our lives" and trying only "the lesser feat of making sense of the ways we try to make sense of our lives,"[2] thinking there is only our choosing and our telling of stories. I have to find a thoroughfare, if I can, an unobstructed way, if there is one, passing between the arbitrary and the inevitable, passing by the dread of pure chance as well as the despair of pure fate.

I have questions of my own I want to answer, about the time of my life, about love and friendship, about God, questions as to what I may hope, as in the words of the Psalm, "And now, Lord, what is there to wait for? In you rests all my hope."[3] If I can find my way between chance and fate, between dread and despair, I can see a light and feel a presence here too in human affairs. I can find God; I can find love and friendship; I can find time.

A TIMELESS PRESENCE IN TIME

There is something that happens to time in stories, as if time were altogether relative, the beginning in an indefinite past, "Once upon a time . . .," the ending in an indefinite future, " . . . and they lived happily ever after," the middle in an indefinite present where many years can pass in what seems a single day, as in *The Golden Key*, and a single day can last for what seems many years. There is something here that touches a deep wish within us, something that touches me as I wonder about the time of my life, if I have much or little time to live, about love and friendship, if they are lasting or passing, about God, if I am to enter into a more heart-to-heart relation with God while I live. I feel again the deep longing of the man in *The Green Child* "to escape from the sense of time, to live in the eternity of what he was accustomed to call 'the divine essence of things,' "[4] to live in the essence of life, to live in love and in friendship, to live heart-to-heart with God.

Shall I trust a longing, though, "to escape from the sense of time"? Is not such a longing tantamount to a wish to escape from reality? Shall I not rather face the reality of time, face my own aging and dying, face the passing of love and friendship in my life, face my aloneness? Facing reality is a kind of seeing. It can becoming a kind of madness, "the madness of the day," as Maurice Blanchot calls it, *la folie du jour*, a living in the blinding light of day. The story he tells of a man seeing in this fashion is a story of madness, a brief story, since there is little to tell, essentially a story of seeing without feeling, of seeing separated from feeling, of a man who is separated from his seeing by someone throwing crushed glass in his eyes, who sees nevertheless the time of life and death, "the day," without any feeling that would make sense of it, who sees therefore its "madness." The story ends, significantly for me, with the words "A story? No. No stories, never again."[5]

If seeing without feeling leads to madness, seeing conjoined with feeling leads to wisdom. If the one leads to seeing "the madness of the day," the other leads to seeing time as "a changing image of eternity." It is feeling that makes the difference, a feeling that can make sense of living and dying, of lasting and passing, of being with others and being alone. There is a wisdom in stories, maybe even a glimpse of Holy Wisdom herself, that conjoins seeing and feeling and keeps one from "the madness of the day" that comes of seeing without feeling, a wisdom that also serves "to keep one's mind clear from the passions that take hold of crowds"[6] that come of the equal and opposite condition, of feeling without seeing. It is the relativity of time as "a changing image of eternity" that appears in "Once upon a time . . ." and " . . . they lived happily ever after" and in a single day that lasts many years and many years that pass in a single day. *What is the divine essence of things?* That is the question I have to ask if I am going to look for wisdom in stories, if I am going to let stories teach me how to conjoin seeing and feeling.

An answer to my questions about the time of my life, about love and friendship, about God would have to be something like "the madness of the day," only "the day" without "the madness," the dayspring, I will say, as in the words "the dayspring from on high hath visited us,"[7] the dayspring of life, of love and friendship, of heart-to-heart. Somehow I have to go from the bare present ("I see this day, and outside it there is nothing") to a presence in the present, a presence in which I can live without living in fear of death, without living in despair of love.

A dayspring is a dawn, the beginning of day, of a new era, of a new order of things, as in the words "the night is far spent, the day is at hand,"[8] the words that moved Augustine in his moment of conversion. They move me too, but I am thinking I have little time to live, my life is far spent, the life after life is at hand. Maybe their meaning for me too, though, is a call to life more than a forewarning of death, a call as in the parables of Jesus, "And what I say unto you I say unto all, Watch!"[9] I am still thinking of the time of my life, as I hear this word of warning, thinking I must watch, keep awake, that is, or death will take me at unawares. "Watch!" does not speak of the coming of death, though, does not call me into living awake in the present moment, but calls me into living awake in a presence, "Watch and pray!" I think of Brother Lawrence in his moment of awakening, seeing a dry and leafless tree in winter and knowing it would put forth leaves in spring, would blossom and bear fruit. The tree is like one of the parables of Jesus. I am that tree! I can see the illumining, feel the kindling, as I contemplate the image. I can see the light, feel the warmth—it is the presence of God!

No doubt, it is one thing to live simply in the present moment and another to live actually in a presence. "I see this day, and outside it there is nothing. Who could take that away from me?", it is said in *The Madness of the Day*. "And when this day fades, I will fade along with it—a thought, a certainty, that enraptures me."[10] So there is knowledge of things passing even when you live in the present, not simple unawareness of past and future. Still, there is something missing here, implied in those words about the day, "and outside it there is nothing," not that I want to say there is something outside the day, outside the present, as if the past still or the future already existed. Rather I want to say there is something inside it, a light, a warmth, a presence, there when you are a dry and leafless tree in winter, that will make you put forth leaves in spring, blossom and bear fruit, something that has to do, therefore, with the past and the future, that draws you nonetheless into the present, so you don't "look back," so you "take no thought for the morrow."

What is it? A light, a warmth, a presence, something that does have to do, after all, with the time of life, yet draws you into its own eternity. It is the presence of eternity, a timeless presence in time. Does it answer my question, though, does it say I have much or little time to live? It seems to answer as in stories, much time, for a single day can last for many years, little time, for many years can pass in a single day.

If I let myself be drawn into eternity in time, I am liable to lose my sense of time, as people do in stories, thinking much time has passed in little or little in much. I am entering into God's time where "one day is as a thousand years and a thousand years as one day."[11] I am losing the sense of time where a day is a day and no more, where many years are many years and no less, but I am not losing the sense of being on a journey with God in time. Maybe this is what it means "not to look back" and "to take no thought for the morrow," to be on a journey, the past behind me, the future ahead of me, and God at my side. "From that moment I have known what it means 'not to look back' and 'to take no thought for the morrow,' " Dag Hammarskjold says, speaking of the moment when he answered "Yes to Someone—or Something," when he said "For all that has been—Thanks! To all that shall be—Yes!"[12] Maybe this is my answer to my own question, to say Yes to the Now of eternity, coming with me out of the past, going with me into the future.

When I think of my past, of love and friendship in my life, and look to the future, asking myself if love is lasting, if friendship is lasting, I am looking back, I can see, I am taking thought for the morrow. What then is "the divine essence" of love and friendship, I wonder, that I may live in its eternity? Again the image of the tree comes to mind, dry and leafless in the winter. It is a human being, loveless and friendless. If I see with eyes like Brother Lawrence's, if I feel with a heart like his, I know the tree will put forth leaves in the spring, will blossom and bear fruit, I know the human being too has a capacity to come to life again, to blossom and bear fruit in love and friendship. Somewhere in there, in that capacity, I believe, is "the divine essence" and "the eternity" I am seeking. I am the tree, the human being. There is a season for love and friendship, and there is a season to be loveless and friendless, I can say, echoing the wisdom of Koheleth, "For everything there is a season, and a time for every matter under heaven."[13] Yet there is something that is for all seasons, the human being, the "I am," who is hidden in unloving, unloved, unlovely life, who is revealed in love and friendship.

There is wisdom in knowing "there is a season, and a time for every matter under heaven," even a season to be loveless and friendless, although it seems so obvious and so commonplace, knowing there is a season also of love and friendship. It is wisdom because it can be there even in a loveless and friendless time, because it is for all seasons. That is the essential thing, I am beginning to believe, that it is for all seasons, for living in it means living therefore in an eternity, in a timeless presence. It means living in touch with the roots of love and friendship even when there is no love and there are no friends, rather than pulling up the roots, turning away from love and friendship in despair. It is wisdom, even Wisdom herself, keeping me company when I am alone.

I encounter "the madness of the day," nevertheless, seeing the time of my life without the feeling of love and friendship to make sense of my life. In fact, it is thought to be wisdom simply to see the madness, as in the opening and closing words of Koheleth, "Vanity of vanities! All is vanity."[14] What is more, the madness runs deep, affecting not only my life but also my times, as in the words "Every man for himself and God against all," the title of a screenplay by Werner Herzog, *Jeder für sich und Gott gegen alle.* The story, as Herzog tells it, is of a foundling, now a young man, who has been kept all his life in confinement, then let out into the world, his impressions and his visions, an unfinished story, an unfinished journey, like the carriage at the end of the play that comes swiftly upon the scene to take on three passengers and then, once they are aboard, does not move off but stands utterly still. "The oarsman sat quietly and praised the journey," Herzog says in the epigraph, and so the foundling says too, toward the end, "Yesterday it was quiet, so I went in the canoe; and the oarsman sat still, praising the voyage."[15]

It is wisdom, seeing the madness, seeing "Every man for himself and God against all"; it is not Wisdom herself, though, I believe, until seeing is conjoined with feeling, until the oarsman sits quietly and praises the journey. Seeing is knowing our aloneness, knowing we are alone and God does not make us unalone. Seeing conjoined with feeling is understanding; I come by way of compassion from knowing to understanding. It is only then, when I feel compassion for those I know and for myself in our aloneness, that I realize I have been living in a hibernation of feeling, a winter of heart and soul. As feeling awakens, as my winter passes, my heart changes and I come to understand it and all hearts. It is only then I praise the journey, my own and that of all, praise it still unfinished as it is.

"God against all" is linked with "Every man for himself," as loving God is linked with loving your neighbor as yourself. If seeing without feeling leaves me isolated, I ask myself, then does seeing conjoined with feeling bring me heart-to-heart with God? I say "heart-to-heart" as if to say "face-to-face," thinking of feeling as well as seeing. Let me try and find an answer to this question too, contemplating the image of the tree, dry and leafless in winter. Only this time I will contemplate also the figure of Brother Lawrence looking at the tree, seeing it will come to life again in spring. There are two figures, therefore, the tree and the human being. The tree will indeed come to life in spring, but Brother Lawrence comes to life on the spot. He is so moved that he falls in love with God and lives the rest of his very simple life ever aware of God's presence, glad to spend his time, as he says, simply picking up straws for God. He has entered into a heart-to-heart relation with God, but the relation is timeless, as if there were no more journey. The experience "had perfectly set him loose from the world," he says in a conversation set down in writing, "and kindled in him such a love for God that he could not tell whether it had increased during the more than forty years he had lived since."[16]

I am taken aback by the timelessness, as if there were no more journey with God in time. Maybe it is simply God's time, though, like the time of stories, "more than forty years" as if it were a single day, a single day as if it were "more than forty years." It is my own life, that single day, those many years, a day as in the literal meaning of the word *journey*, a day's travel, many years as in the years of my lifelong pilgrimage in time. If I step into God's time, I am stepping into a story, into the time of an adventure, into not out of a journey. Maybe this is what it means for the oarsman to sit quietly and praise the journey, to realize it is your own life, to love a story, to rejoice in timeless time.

Is God's time then only something we spin out in the telling of stories? Time, I want to say, is "a changing image of eternity." It appears as an image in the work of imagination, in storytelling. There is, nevertheless, something over and above the image itself, over and above the story, and that is "insight into image."[17] Eternity comes to light in an insight into the changing image that time is, like Brother Lawrence seeing the tree in winter, knowing it will come to life in spring, seeing thereby and feeling a timeless presence in time. There is a revealing of God's heart here, the revealing of a love that is lasting, that is not passing like human love and friendship, a love that is timeless and yet heart-to-heart, that comes from before the beginning of time and reaches on beyond the end of time, a love not only "strong as death,"[18] like human love according to the Song of Solomon, but stronger than death, the love that made the tree of the cross, dry and leafless in the winter of death, put forth leaves, blossom and bear fruit in the spring of resurrection.

If time is "a changing image of eternity," then time is always telling us of eternity. Or eternity is always speaking to us through time. I think of the young woman Viktor Frankl met in the death camp who used to spend time looking at a tree outside her window, sometimes even talking with the tree. When asked if the tree ever said anything to her, she answered that it did, that it said "I am here—I am here—I am life, eternal life!"[19] When I ask myself what God is saying to me through the changing time of my life, I believe it must be that very thing, "I am here—I am here—I am life, eternal life!" I think too of Jesus in the Gospel of John, of Simon Peter saying to him "You have the words of eternal life!"[20] Words are being spoken to me, I do believe, and they are being spoken heart-to-heart, but their message is so pure and simple that it is easy for me to pay no attention, easy to think nothing at all is being said.

I am a presence, we are a presence, God is a presence in time. So if time is "a changing image of eternity," the presence of eternity is God and us, God among us. It is the inverse of "Every man for himself and God against all." It is what Jesus calls "the kingdom of god," what he is announcing when he says

"The kingdom of God is at hand!"[21] It is the subject of his parables, the point of his warning, "Watch!" When I wonder about the time of my life, whether I have much or little time to live, I am not thinking of my presence, of our presence, of God's presence, but of time in and of itself. Words that challenge the absolute reign of time, therefore, that speak of the reign of God, are "words of eternal life" for me. And as I do begin to think of presence, I begin to think of time as a transparent medium rather like the water of a stream than as something ultimate like the rock bottom. I begin to see how my life, my own presence in time, is significant apart from much or little time to live.

We are a presence in time, and our presence is what Martin Buber calls "I and thou." It is what Kant calls "a kingdom of ends,"[22] a moral kingdom of persons. If time is "a changing image of eternity," we are a presence of eternity to one another. I am struck, thinking of the parable of the tree, by what Buber says of having a relation with a tree, of going from "I and it" to "I and thou" with a tree.[23] Once I had a friend who used to commune with trees, who used to stand in front of a tree as if in conversation. I was never near enough, I say now as I tell the story to make people smile, to know what he was saying or what the tree was saying to him. I do it myself now, though, acting out the parable of the tree, knowing it is a way of practicing the presence of eternity. It is healing, I find, when love and friendship seem passing, for it seems to say "I and thou" remain, the roots of love and friendship remain, even when lover and friend, even when intimacy has passed away.

God is a presence in time, while the time of my life passes, while our intimacy with one another passes, "the eternal thou"[24] in love and in death. It is by relationship with God that I too am eternal, although the time of my life is passing, that we too are eternal, although our intimacy with one another is passing. It is like stepping inside the hollow of a living tree, something I have done among the giant redwoods, being inside a living being. I am inside, all those who belong to my life are inside, surrounded by goodness and mercy. It is like being inside a story, inside a song.

What is the story? What is the song? That is the question of what time is telling us of eternity. A story can be told, a song can be sung even while our journey is still underway. We can sit quietly and praise the journey. I wonder what a sage would say, though, what Wisdom herself would say to the dilemmas of our lives and times. Maybe it would be enough to say we are able to choose, what is happening is not irresistible, it is not foolhardy to oppose it, to say on the other hand there is more to it than our choosing and our storytelling, there is a hidden presence, there is a meaning in unmeaning things of life. To say only this of war and of peace, for instance, to say it of famine and of abundance, of sickness and of health, of death and of life, would be to open our eyes, to kindle our hearts even while we stand on the verge of apocalypse.

A MEANING IN UNMEANING THINGS OF LIFE

A revealing of eternity in time, an "apocalypse," that is, a "revelation," would be a revealing of presence, of our presence and of God's presence among us. I think of the Apocalypse at the end of the New Testament, but I read it as the revealing of "a kingdom of ends," of God's presence in time and of our presence to one another—the very word *parousia* means "presence." I think of children's games of hiding and revealing, the hiding and seeking and finding in a game of hide-and-seek, the covering and uncovering of eyes in a game of blindman's bluff. I think especially of something that is not yet fully a game, very young children trying to hide themselves by covering their own eyes with their hands and then to reveal themselves by taking their hands away. For if I am a presence and we are a presence and God is a presence in time, the revealing of person to person is in eyes meeting eyes and in hearts meeting hearts.

It is true, "a kingdom of ends," a kingdom of persons, of ends rather than means, is not the same as an ending, especially an ending in death and destruction. I think of ring-around-a-rosy, a children's singing game where the players dance around in a circle and then squat or fall down:

> Ring around a rosy,
> Pocket full of posy—

Ashes, ashes,
We all fall down![25]

It is an ominous game, this one, a dance of death. Games like this of ending, nevertheless, as well as those of hiding and revealing, point to something true, the games of ending to a life ending in death, the games of hiding and revealing to the persons who live the life, who are hidden and revealed in living and in dying.

If I put the two truths together, a life ending in death and the person who is living the life, a time passing away and the people who are living in the time, I can find a meaning in my life and my times. Meaning is in the conjunction, I believe, of the long perspectives of ending and the eternal presence of persons. Those questions I have been asking about the time of my life, about love and friendship, about God, if I turn them into questions about my times, become questions about an ending of time, about "a kingdom of ends," about a kingdom of God. If I say "Things are meant," speaking of the things of my life, I am saying things belong to my life, considering them in relation to me the person who am living my life. If I say "Things are meant," speaking of my times, I am saying things belong to my times, considering them in relation to the spiritual world of persons who are living in my times. "I can put it no plainer than by saying that Bilbo was *meant* to find the Ring, and *not* by its maker," Gandalf says in Tolkien's story of the magic ring. "In which case you also were *meant* to have it. And that may be an encouraging thought."[26]

"It is not," Frodo answers. "Though I am not sure that I understand you." To be "meant" in Tolkien's story is to be intended. To be "meant," as I am using the word, is to belong to the story of a life or a time, to be meaningful as things are, to have meaning as things do in a story. It is taking one more step then to say things seen in the long perspectives of ending and in the eternal presence of persons belong to a journey with God. If I take this step, as I am going to now, to see how encouraging it may be, to see how I may come to understand it, I am saying meaning is something I discover rather than something I invent.

War, famine, pestilence, death, the Four Horsemen of the Apocalypse, are at large in our times, and their power over the human spirit, like that of the ghostly horsemen in Tolkien's story, is in terror and despair.[27] These two, terror and despair, I believe, are the demonic forces at work in our times. Here is where we need the wisdom that not only keeps one from "the madness of the day," from seeing without feeling, but is also able "to keep one's mind clear of the passions that take hold of crowds," of feeling without seeing, of being caught up in terror and despair. It is a wisdom I come upon in telling the story of my journey with God in time. Here again I think of the image of the tree, only now it is an evergreen tree, a giant redwood tree, one of the oldest living beings on earth. To be in the presence of a living being so old, whose story goes back into time out of mind, somehow takes away the madness of seeing without feeling as well as the terror and despair of feeling without seeing. It is like being in the presence of God. Indeed, to walk with God, I begin to think, is to conjoin seeing and feeling, to find meaning in otherwise unmeaning things of life, to live in time out of mind.

It is truly "out of mind" for us, God's time, immemorial in the direction of the past, unknown in the direction of the future. A meaning comes to light for us in the present, nevertheless, when we see and feel the present moment in the eternal presence. I think of the moment in *The Golden Key* when Tangle comes upon the Ancient Child playing upon the mossy floor of a deep cavern, playing with little balls that he sets out in strange geometric figures ("Time is a child playing," Heraclitus says). "And now Tangle felt there was something in her knowledge which was not in her understanding."[28] It is the same for us with the meaning of the things of our life and our times. There is something in our knowledge which is not yet in our understanding, but as we watch the Ancient Child playing, something happens for us as for Tangle, "an indescribable vague intelligence went on rousing itself in her mind," until like her we break in upon the play and ask the child to guide us.

What is there in the play of time, in what happens, that could be in our knowledge and not yet in our understanding? "For she knew there must be an infinite meaning in the changes and sequences and individual forms of the figures into which the child arranged the balls, as well as the varied harmonies of their colours," it is said of Tangle, "but what it all meant she could not tell."[29] So it is for us. We know there must be an infinite meaning in the things that happen in our lives and times, or we may believe or hope there is, but what it all means we cannot tell. I can know "Things are meant" and not yet understand what the meaning is. Say a chance meeting with another person occurs that affects the course of my life. If "all real living is meeting,"[30] I can expect to find a meaning here. I can expect to find "I and thou," or at least the possibility of "I and thou," in all the conjunctions of lives that occur in the play of time.

As I watch the conjunction and disjunction of lives in the play of time, I find meaning and unmeaning. I find unmeaning rather in the disjunction, especially in the separations that occur in war and famine and sickness and death. "A little child shall lead them,"[31] Isaiah says of the time when wolf and lamb, leopard and kid, lion and calf shall dwell together in peace, the very opposite, as it seems, of our times when the Four Horsemen are still at large. Maybe the solution is Tangle's act of breaking in upon the play and asking the Ancient Child to lead her. As long as I am merely watching the play of time, I see what Koheleth sees, "For everything there is a season, and a time for every matter under heaven," a time of war and a time of peace, a time of famine and a time of abundance, a time of sickness and a time of health, a time of death and a time of life. I see the living and the dying, the meeting and the parting. I see "a changing image of eternity," changing always from opposite to opposite. If I am unwilling, though, simply to continue watching, if I break in upon the play and ask the Ancient Child to guide me, I am trying to go from "a changing image" to "insight into image." There is a peace in the child's demeanor, like the peace I find in the presence of the ancient trees, that draws me to ask for guidance, a peace that is greater and more encompassing than the peace that is the opposite of war, a peace that belongs to the timelessness of eternity.,

"There was such an awfulness of absolute repose on the face of the child that Tangle stood dumb before him," but by the end of the story, when Mossy and Tangle meet again, man and woman, after having long been parted, her face too is "as still and peaceful"[32] as that of the Ancient Child. Here is what I want for myself, to live in the peace I find in the presence of God, to meet other persons in that peace, to meet again in that peace after having been parted from one another. "He had no smile," it is said of the Ancient Child, "but the love in his large grey eyes was deep as the center." To live in deep-running stillness, I have to live clear down in my heart. Living clear is seeing; living in your heart is feeling; living clear down in your heart is seeing conjoined with feeling. Clear down is "deep as the center." Here is my answer to the madness of seeing without feeling, to the terror and despair of feeling without seeing. It is the madness that separates us, the terror and the despair.

If I am living clear down in my heart, I am living already in "a kingdom of ends," a spiritual world of persons, but if I am to conjoin seeing and feeling, I have to go further than Kant himself did, I have to conjoin the two realms he left separate, "the starry heavens above me and the moral law within me."[33] Here again the image of the child playing is helpful. It is as if the game the child is playing, the play of time, represents "the starry heavens above me" as well as "the moral law within me." Time is something human, a human measure, and so it measures humanly not only our human existence but also the existence of the universe in which we live, not only our relations with one another but also our relations with the universe. As a game of chance, the play of time is a game in which the chances of life determine the outcome of our lives, in which the universe, as it were, decides our lives. As a game of skill, it is a game in which our own abilities determine the outcome, in which we ourselves decide. As a game being played by the Ancient Child, though, a figure of Wisdom, it is a "pastime," a way of passing the time of our lives, that is, in which neither mere chance nor mere skill determine our lives, in which we follow instead the leading of Wisdom.

As a play of chance, our meetings and partings, the conjunctions and disjunctions of our lives, are only the chances of life, the things that happen in the course of human life. As a play of skill, they are the result of fundamental decisions we have made as to how we shall live. As a play of Wisdom, though, they are the enactment in time of our relationship with eternity, an enacting of our relationship with ourselves, with one another, and with God, a free enacting of an "I and thou" that is eternal. Thus in the play of Wisdom the universe has a role, the "I and thou" is eternal; and we have a role, the "I and thou" is freely enacted; the spiritual world of persons is eternal and yet it is freely enacted in time. I am thinking here of what Kierkegaard calls "the moment,"[34] when you freely enact your relationship with eternity, only I am extending the idea from the individual to the whole world of persons.

It is an insight to go from seeing the play of Wisdom as having to do only with the realm of "pure reason," Kant's term, to seeing it as having to do also with that of "practical reason," from seeing it as having to do only with "speculative judgment" as to the truth of "divine things," as Aquinas did at first, to seeing it as having to do also with "practical judgment" as to how we shall relate to "divine things," as he ultimately did[35]— it is tantamount to going from pure seeing to seeing conjoined with feeling. When I am simply watching what is happening, reading the daily newspaper, for instance, seeing the ravages of war and famine and pestilence and death, I am concerned about the power and goodness of God, and thus about "divine things," wondering "Is God able to avert evil things from happening to us? Is it God's will to avert evil from happening?" When I go from contemplation to action, though, breaking in upon the play of time and asking the guidance of Wisdom, I am seeing the power and goodness of God in terms of their free enactment by us in time, as if "Thy will be done on earth as it is in heaven" comes true in our doing of God's will on earth. Once I heard a child, three years, old, ask the simple question, "Why doesn't God feed the poor people?" It took me an entire week to think of the equally simple answer, "Because God wants us to feed them."

When "the moment" comes, therefore, when we freely enact our relationship with eternity, then comes the kingdom of God. It is true, time is already "a changing image of eternity"; the play of time is a sequence of occasion after occasion to enact our relationship with eternity. Each occasion is a human situation where I am present, where we are present, where God is present. When I forget who is present, I can fall into the madness of seeing without feeling, into the terror and the despair of feeling without seeing. It is when I remember, it is then "the moment" comes. Say I see my own life passing. Say I see my own powerlessness to change the course of my times away from war and famine and pestilence and death. Say I feel the terror of losing all I now cherish, the despair of being able to do anything about it. Say I remember then my presence, our presence, God's presence. It is then I am "not far from the kingdom of God."[36]

My presence, when I see it as eternity shining in time, means my life is significant, even though my life is passing, even though I am unable to avert the evils of my times. For I have a relationship with eternity and I am able to enact my relationship in time and thus to enact the significance of everything I do and of everything that happens to me. There is my power—to enact the meaning of what happens. The meaning is there in my resolving of "the problems of the human heart in conflict with itself," as William Faulkner calls them, something that must not be overshadowed, he says, either in the living of life or in the telling of stories by "a general and universal physical fear so long sustained by now that we can even bear it,"[37] the terror and the despair of war and famine and pestilence and death in our times. Something eternal comes to light in this, "the human heart in conflict with itself" as I experience it is my life, eternal because it is not overshadowed by "a general and universal physical fear" in my times. Thus I set my life over and against my times, and I am alone, but I set it alongside all other lives, and I am unalone.

Our presence then, when I set my life alongside other lives, when I realize I am unalone, means there is hope of knowing and being known, of loving and being loved, where I thought there was no hope, where I thought I was confined within the solitude of my own heart. As I look through my diary of these past years, I find myself again and again searching for some new myth, some new story in which to see my own life, as if I were trapped in a myth of aloneness, caught in a story that does confine me within the solitude of my own heart, as if I were at the mercy of the time spirit (*Zeitgeist*) according to which a human being is ultimately an island. That is the upshot, I believe, of what I am calling "the demonic forces" at work in our times, the madness of seeing without feeling, the terror and the despair of feeling without seeing—to isolate us from one another, to make islands of us. I find the myth I am looking for, the story I want to live in, where I find human beings able to meet in their aloneness, where I find "the human heart in conflict with itself" slowly change into "heart speaks to heart," very slowly as in Austin Tappan Wright's *Islandia*, the story of a man finding the basis, the common ground, for a relationship with a woman. "When I first came here, I thought sometimes that I would die because of the silence and a loneliness that is in the very air itself," he tells her in the story. "For me that loneliness proved to be an anteroom to a more vivid reality than I had ever known before. One has to be lonely first."[38]

God's presence, missing in Wright's story, takes away the sadness in the silence, in the loneliness, takes away the sadness that lingers even in "a more vivid reality." God's presence for me is a well-being I find in the being of things, in the being of the ancient trees, in the being of a tree barren in winter and flourishing again in spring, in the play of time as "a changing image of eternity," in the being of human beings. That for me is "the divine essence of things." If I were saying with Eckhart "God is existence," I would say it is simply the existence of things; if I were saying with Gandhi "God is truth," I would say it is simply the truth of things; but saying as I am "God is life and light and love," I will say it is *the well-being of things*, the well-being of human and of all living beings:

There was such an awfulness of absolute repose on the face of the child that Tangle stood dumb before him. He had no smile, but the love in his large grey eyes was deep as the center. And with the repose there lay on his face a shimmer as of moonlight, which seemed as if any moment it might break into such a ravishing smile as would cause the beholder to weep himself to death. But the smile never came, and the moonlight lay there unbroken. For the heart of the child was too deep for any smile to reach from it to his face.[39]

My way out of being an island, accordingly, my story of us meeting in our aloneness, is really a story of God, a story like that of Mossy and Tangle, man and woman meeting again after seeing the child's play of time, after feeling the well-being that is deeper than any smile, after coming to understand "the heart of the child." There is a seeing, there is a feeling, and there is a conjoining of seeing and feeling in understanding. I see the play of time, the joy of our meeting, and the sorrow of our parting, and yet I feel a well-being that is deeper than our joy and our sorrow, and so I come to understand, or at least to glimpse in understanding, the heart of the Divine Child, to know there is a well-being that is deeper than our fortune and our misfortune, even as God is deeper, and to know the well-being is nevertheless ours, even as God is ours.

Asking my questions about the time of my life, about love and friendship, about God, I am like Tangle asking the child "Can you tell me the way to the country the shadows fall from?"[40] I am asking really about the kingdom of my presence, of our presence, of God's presence. It is I, it is we, it is God who casts the shadows. It is a timeless presence in time, mine, ours, God's. The shadows are the many images of eternity that are formed in the play of time. If I walk with God, I am like Tangle walking with the child, holding the child's hand and yet being led by the child. When I see my presence, our presence, God's presence in the long perspectives of time, I see a journey ahead of us, enacting the eternal presence in time, enacting the kingdom of God. It is a meaning in otherwise unmeaning things of life we are enacting. I wanted to say I discover, I do not invent the meaning. What I have learned now, though, meditating on presence and on meaning, is that I do something in between discovering and inventing—I enact.

I can see there are far-reaching consequences of what I am saying now (about enacting), especially when I think of Karl Marx setting action over and against contemplation. "All mysteries which mislead theory to mysticism," Marx says, "find their rational solution in human practice and in the comprehension of this practice."[41] Is wisdom to be found in contemplation, I ask myself, or is it to be found in action? There is something to be discovered, I do believe, something for contemplation, and there is something to be enacted, something for action. There are mysteries, simple and elemental, my presence to myself, our presence to one another, God's presence to us, and they do lead to mysticism, to an experience of light and presence. There is also human practice, my enacting of my relationship with eternity, our enacting of our relationship with one another, the enacting of a relationship with God, and there is the comprehension of this practice, my grasping of the meaning there is in the enacting, a meaning otherwise unrealized. Wisdom, I conclude, is not contemplation alone, not action alone, but contemplation in action. It is the realization of meaning.

I can feel the well-being, nevertheless, that is already present and at work in time, present in God's presence, in our presence, in my presence. "Why do you not think of him as the coming one," Rilke says of God, "imminent from all eternity, the future one, the final fruit of the tree whose leaves we are?"[42] Because the sap of God's presence is already flowing in the trees, I want to answer. Because the final fruit is not God, only God, but the kingdom of God. Because we are the tree, and our putting forth leaves, our blossoming, our bearing fruit is our realizing of eternity in time.

Still, God *is* "the coming one, imminent from all eternity, the future one, the final fruit of the tree whose leaves we are," God for us, that is, God among us. It is "the human heart in conflict with itself" that brings on the coming of God, I believe, as it changes into "heart speaks to heart," as it comes to know itself in a heart-to-heart with God. Thus the message of Jesus, "Repent, for the kingdom of heaven is at hand!"[43] "Repent!" means "Change your hearts!" It is a kingdom of hearts, "the kingdom of heaven," a kingdom of light and of presence. It is "at hand" even now, if *parousia* means "presence," if the coming is a revealing. Apocalypse in our times is a revealing, I expect, "that thoughts out of many hearts may be revealed,"[44] that thoughts of my own heart may be revealed to me, that thoughts of our hearts may be revealed one to another, that thoughts of God's heart may be revealed to us. What thoughts? I think again of the heart of a child, of the figure of Wisdom as a woman, of the figure of Wisdom as a child, of the woman playing before God at the beginning of time, of the child playing at the end of time, of the well-being in that playing, and I think there is a well-being that is deeper than madness, deeper than terror and despair.

NOTES

1. Bernard Berenson, quoted by Isaiah Berlin, *Historical Inevitability* (London: Oxford University Press, 1957), p. 3.
2. Frank Kermode, *The Sense of an Ending* (London: Oxford University Press, 1967), p. 3.
3. Psalm 39:7 from *The New American Bible* (Washington, D.C.: Confraternity of Christian Doctrine, 1970).
4. Herbert Read, *The Green Child* (New York: New Directions, 1948), p. 12.
5. Maurice Blanchot, *The Madness of the Day/La folie du jour*, trans. Lydia David (Barrytown, N.Y.: Station Hill, 1981), p. 18. The French is "*Un récit? Non, pas de récit, plus jamais,*" p. 31.
6. Padriac Colum, *Storytelling New and Old* (New York: Macmillan, 1968), p. 20.
7. Luke 1:78 (King James Version).
8. Romans 13:12 (King James Version).
9. Mark 13:37 (King James Version), cf. 14:38 ("Watch and pray").
10. Blanchot, *The Madness of the Day*, p. 6.
11. 2 Peter 3:8.
12. Dag Hammarskjold, *Markings*, trans. Leif Sjoberg and W. H. Auden (New York: Knopf, 1964), pp. 205 and 89, alluding to Luke 9:62 ("No one who puts his hand to the plow and looks back is fit for the kingdom of God.") and Matthew 6:34 ("Take no thought for the morrow" in King James Version).
13. Koheleth (Ecclesiastes) 3:1.
14. Koheleth 1:2 and 12:8.
15. Werner Herzog, "Every Man for Himself and God Against All" in his *Screenplays*, trans. Alan Greenberg and Martje Herzog (New York: Tanam, 1980), pp. 97 and 172.
16. Brother Lawrence (Nicolas Herman), *The Practice of the Presence of God* (Mt. Vernon, N.Y.: Peter Pauper Press, 1963), p. 5.
17. Cf. Bernard Lonergan, *Insight* (London: Longmans, 1961).
18. Song of Solomon 8:6.
19. Viktor Frankl, *Man's Search for Meaning*, trans. Ilse Lasch (Boston: Beacon, 1962), p. 69.
20. John 6:68.
21. Mark 1:15.
22. Immanuel Kant, *The Metaphysic of Ethics*, trans. Thomas Kingsmill Abott (London: Longmans, 1916), pp. 68–69.
23. Martin Buber, *I and Thou*, trans. Ronald Gregor Smith (New York: Scribner's, 1958), pp. 7–8.
24. Ibid, pp. 6 and 101.
25. I am quoting the version I have heard children using. It may be a corruption of this one used in England:

    A ring, a ring of roses,
    A pocketful of posies—
    Ashem, ashem, all fall down.

    Cf. Alice Bertha Gomme, *The Traditional Games of England, Scotland, and Ireland*, vol. 2 (London: David Nutt, 1898), p. 110. The word *Ashem* is supposed to be a sound of sneezing. There has been speculation about this game having originated at the time of the Plague—the sneezing and coughing of the pneumonic plague—considered doubtful by Iona and Peter Opie in *The Oxford Dictionary of Nursery Rhymes* (Oxford: Clarendon, 1952), p. 365.

26. J. R. R. Tolkien, *The Lord of the Rings*, one-volume edition (London: George Allen & Unwin, 1969), p. 69.
27. Apocalypse (Revelation) 6:2–8. Cf. Tolkien, *The Lord of the Rings*, pp. 190 ("their power is in terror") and 855 ("dread and despair").
28. George MacDonald, *The Golden Key* (New York: Farrar, Straus & Giroux, 1967), p. 60. Cf. Heraclitus, Fragment 52, in Herman Diels and Walther Kranz, *Die Frangmente der Vorsokratiker* (Berlin: Weidmann, 1934), 1:162, and my discussion in *The Way of All the Earth* (New York: Macmillan, 19721), p. 154 and in *Time and Myth* (Garden City, N.Y.: Doubleday, 1973), p. 3.
29. MacDonald, ibid. Here MacDonald adds a footnote, "I think I must be indebted to Novalis for these geometric figures."
30. Buber, *I and Thou*, p. 11.
31. Isaiah 11:6.
32. MacDonald, *The Golden Key*, pp. 73–74.
33. Kant, *Critique of Practical Reason*, trans. Lewis White Beck (Chicago: University of Chicago Press, 1949), p. 258.
34. Sören Kierkegaard, *Philosophical Fragments*, trans. David Swenson and Howard Hong (Princeton, N.J.: Princeton University Press, 1962), pp. 16–26. Cf. my discussion in *The Way of All the Earth*, pp. 136–155.
35. Cf. how Aquinas changes his mind on the gifts of the Holy Spirit of understanding and wisdom and knowledge and counsel in his *Summa Theologiae*, from I–II q. 68 a. 4 to II–II q. 8 a. 6.
36. Mark 12:34.
37. William Faulkner, Nobel Address in *The Faulkner Reader* (New York: Random House, 1954), p. 3.
38. Austin Tappan Wright, *Islandia* (New York: Farrar & Rinehart, 1942), p. 876.
39. MacDonald, *The Golden Key*, p. 61.
40. Ibid, p. 62.
41. Karl Marx, *Theses on Feuerbach*, Thesis 8, in Karl Marx and Friedrich Engels, *Basic Writings on Politics and Philosophy*, ed. Lewis S. Feuer (Garden City, N.Y.: Doubleday, 1959), p. 245.
42. Rainer Maria Rilke, *Letters to a Young Poet*, trans. M. D. Herter Norton (New York: Norton, 1962), p. 49.
43. Matthew 4:17.
44. Luke 2:35.

4. "There are signs"

on going from station
to station in the Rothko Chapel

Seeing a light in my life and times, "dark times" as they have been called, feeling a presence, mine, ours, God's, I look for signs, human configurations, in the changing scene and the persons who come on the scene, like the changing landscape and the persons you meet on a journey, "men in dark times," as Hannah Arendt calls them, speaking really of men and women, whose exists and entrances make the changing scene, as time itself, "a changing image of eternity," whose presence in time is an illumining of minds and a kindling of hearts.

When I say "There are signs," I am thinking of people whose lives illumine the darkness of their times. "You can discern the face of the sky," Jesus says to those who ask him for a sign from heaven, "but can you not discern the signs of the times?"[1] What are "the signs of the times"? John the Baptist, I think, and above all, Jesus himself. There are signs, I want to go on and say, in all times. "Even in the darkest of times we have a right to expect some illumination," Arendt says, "and such illumination may well come less from theories and concepts than from the uncertain, flickering, and often weak light that some men and women, in their lives and works, will kindle under almost all circumstances and shed over the time span that was given them on earth."[2] There are human configurations, the hap and mishap of what is happening, the happiness and unhappiness, I do find, where human beings stand forth not in their fortune and misfortune but in their relation to the eternal in us, to the meaning in what is what in our lives, to the presence in who is who.

Is everyone and everything a sign? There is always a meaning in what is what, always a presence in who is who, but not always the same relation on our part to the meaning and the presence.

At times when I see no meaning in what is happening, when I feel no presence, life can seem to me, as to Macbeth, "a tale told by an idiot, full of sound and fury, signifying nothing."[3] When I do see, when I do feel, I become myself a sign to others while everyone and everything becomes a sign to me. Consider the following configurations: necessity where human beings are facing an inescapable fate, possibility where they have a choice to make, impossibility where they are pursuing an unattainable goal, contingency where they come upon the hap and mishap of life. I think of all these configurations in my own life: facing the prospect of aging and dying, choosing my road in life, pursuing an inexhaustible heart's desire, letting my own luck go with me and guide me while keeping up my heart and going to meet my fortune. I realize, as I consider these attitudes, I am relying on Something beyond what is what, on Someone beyond who is who; I am not just facing and choosing and pursuing and meeting things as they come.

If I take all human configurations this way, as relating to and signifying Something or Someone rather than as "signifying nothing," then I am always being led by life into a greater life, always passing from the day into a greater day. "Christianity 'outruns' the cross,"[4] Roland Barthes says, meaning the reality of Christianity is greater than its symbol the cross. So too the greater life outruns life, the greater day outruns the day. Let me see if I can learn to pass over from human configurations to the reality they signify, if I can run fast enough to catch up with the reality that outruns necessity and possibility and impossibility and contingency.

"Christianity 'outruns' the cross." There is a clue for me in these words. I think of my visits during the last few days to the Rothko Chapel, where I have seen the fourteen somber and almost featureless paintings of Mark Rothko in an octagonal chamber, originally intended to be a Catholic chapel but now used for Jewish, Christian, Muslim, and even Hindu worship. I cannot help but think of the fourteen stations of the cross that are usually to be seen in a Catholic chapel. Instead of the usual images of the events in the passion of Jesus, there is one large canvas in black with a large maroon border underneath and narrow maroon borders on the top and sides corresponding maybe to the principal event, the crucifixion of Jesus, and there are thirteen others, two sets of three in black with maroon borders, another set of three across from the principal one and a single one at each of the four smaller corners in black with a maroon wash, corresponding without distinction to the remaining events. All I could think of several years ago when I first saw the chapel was that Mark Rothko had committed suicide (four years after completing the paintings). I thought I was seeing despair, and all I wanted to do was to get out of there as quickly as I could. Now, after seeing Ayasofya and feeling the encompassing peace I found there, I know I am not seeing despair but some deep insight into human suffering. I feel a peace here as I felt there, as if there were peace to be found in the depths of suffering, a peace "which passes all understanding."[5]

There is indeed a reality here that "outruns" the symbols of suffering, though the outrunning is here somehow in the paintings themselves and in the octagonal space of their setting. There is the breadth of a greater life that lives on through our death, the light of a greater day that shines on in the darkness of our times. Yet the breath is in the still space; the light is in the dark paintings. As I sit here, I too become still, I become illumined. It is as if I were looking for a sign of Something or Someone, and I find it where I least expect, as if I find life and light and love where everything seems barren and dark and cold.

What are the signs of our times? It occurs to me I can find here what I am seeking, I can see in these dark paintings the light shining in the darkness of our times, in these stations of the cross, maybe by actually going from station to station, meditating and praying, as one would in a Catholic chapel. The elimination of all detail in these paintings, the absence of the traditional pictures or images that symbolize the scenes of Christ's passion, is significant, I am sure. Ordinarily the stations would be the following: 1. Jesus is condemned to death; 2. Jesus bears his cross; 3. Jesus falls the first time; 4. Jesus meets his mother; 5. Jesus is helped by Simon; 6. Veronica wipes the face of Jesus; 7. Jesus falls a second time; 8. Jesus speaks to the women of Jerusalem; 9. Jesus falls a third time; 10. Jesus is stripped of his garments; 11. Jesus is nailed to the cross; 12. Jesus dies on the cross (this is the principal station); 13. Jesus is taken down from the cross; 14. Jesus is placed in the tomb. I was going to say there is no one-to-one correspondence here with these scenes, but I have learned Rothko had originally intended to place the numbers of the fourteen stations on the outside of the chapel to show where each panel was located on the inside.[6] The absence of images or pictures on the panels, nevertheless, seems to be essential, to go with the nonrepresentational art of our times, and to speak thus of our times, and to go also with Rothko's background as a Jew and the commandment "You shall not make for yourself a graven image,"[7] and to speak thus of God.

In fact, I begin to realize, the paintings do not show Christ suffering so much as what is seen by the suffering Christ's eyes, what is felt by the suffering Christ's heart. They do not show the men and women of our times so much as what is seen by human eyes and felt by the human heart of our times. If I go from station to station, therefore, I am not going from icon to icon of Christ, from icon to icon of the saints of our times, but from vision to vision of the eyes, from vision to vision of the heart.

"I was always looking for something more,"[8] Rothko says of these paintings. As I begin going from station to station, I find myself doing the same, always looking for something more, looking for life where all is death, looking for light where all is dark, looking for love where all is cold. I begin with the painting of death, the principal one as I imagine, corresponding to the station where Jesus dies on the cross, or maybe it corresponds to the first station where Jesus is condemned to death. Certainly it is the one that stands out most distinctly in this chapel, the beginning and the end of the circle. As I contemplate it, I think of the question a child asked his mother (she told me of this, wondering), "Was Jesus real when he was on the cross?" No doubt, the child was thinking of the crucifixes he had seen, where there is a sculpture of Jesus, an image rather than the reality. His question, nevertheless, is the age-old one of Docetism (I am amazed again, as I think of a child asking this), a Christ who appeared to human beings in a spiritual body, who had no actual human body, who only seemed to suffer and die on the cross. Here in the Rothko painting there is no image of Jesus at all. There is only the image of his experience, if I am right, a retinal image, as it were, of his seeing and his feeling, this hard-edged black rectangle on a maroon field, this window onto a dark world.

"Yes," I say to myself, contemplating this dark world, "he was facing real death and so he was living real life." There are *signs of life* here, I realize, as I make the child's question my own and answer it for myself. When I ask the child's question, "Was Jesus real when he was on the cross?" I put into words something that has been troubling me about Christianity, an uneasiness I felt at the Abbey of Gethsemane, for instance, at the stations of the cross set out all around the grounds there and the life-size representation of the scene where Jesus prays in agony, at those scenes of suffering and death surrounded on all sides by the beauty of the Kentucky hills, an uneasiness really at the emphasis on suffering and death in Christianity, at the contrast of Christianity with the other religions, centering around the passion and death of Christ. It all comes to a head here, this uneasiness of mine, as I gaze on these dark panels, where I do not see a human figure undergoing suffering and death but face myself the suffering and death he was facing, here in this place consecrated not only to Christianity but to all the great religions.

There are signs of life here, breath and warmth and heartbeat, as it were, breath of spirit, warmth of soul, heartbeat of sense, signs of the standpoint I must take to enter into these paintings, a standpoint of the living not of the dead, of one who is alive, though facing death and suffering. As I enter into this standpoint, facing death, looking into this hard-edged rectangle of black as into a mirror that does not reflect my image, I realize I am not facing my dead self but looking into a nothing that is no-thing, into a meaning beyond what is what, into a presence beyond who is who. I had thought of death sometimes as a mirror in which your living self meets your dead self. Yet it is not so. Somehow this speaks to my uneasiness. I am seeing with the eyes and feeling with the heart of a Christ who is alive, though I am seeing no-thing and feeling no-thing.

It is hard to tell no-thing from nothing—thus the uneasiness of Rothko's critics, "Was there anything there at all?"[9] My own uneasiness, about suffering and death in Christianity, begins to resolve when I form my reply, an answer to the child's question from seeing the figure of Jesus, an answer also to the critics' question from seeing no figure, "Yes, he was facing real death and so he was living real life." Real death and real life, they go together, and yet death is no-thing, and life too, though there are things of life, is itself no-thing. All those human configurations I have been considering, facing an inescapable death, choosing a way in life, pursuing an inexhaustible heart's desire, meeting the chances of life, all those modalities of necessity and possibility and impossibility and contingency, are modalities of no-thing, and yet the facing, the choosing, the pursuing, the meeting is nonetheless real. I begin to see and to feel the paradox in which I am standing, life-in-death, the greater life, the encompassing life, the opposite of which is not death but death-in-life, a living death, a life empty of all well-being. Now I can see "the life in him was light."[10]

"We adore thee O Christ and we bless thee," I say in the traditional words, "because by thy holy cross thou hast redeemed the world," and I pass now from station to station around the octagon, seeing the panels that are completely black with a maroon wash as well as those that are rectangles of black on fields of maroon. When I see the maroon wash over black, I think of suffering. When I see the rectangles of black, I think of death. It is hard to tell life-in-death from death-in-life, I reflect, just as it is to tell no-thing from nothing. A life of suffering can seem a living death, a life empty of all well-being, but here it is revealed to be a life that lives on both sides of death. "The true pattern of life extends through both domains," Rilke says, "the blood with the greatest circuit runs through both."[11] There is blood here, in the red (the maroon is a dark red), and there is death, in the black: The two are mixed in the black with the maroon wash, as if life and death were mixed, and they are separated in the black on the field of maroon, as if life and death were separated. There are the two domains, life and death, and so there is the separation, this side and the other side of death, and yet "the blood with the greatest circuit runs through both," the greater life runs through both, and the mixture of life and death on this side is suffering.

I ask myself again the child's question, "Was Jesus real when he was on the cross?" I am asking now, though, if his suffering was real. Here again I am putting into words my own uneasiness, only now it is the other side of focusing upon death and suffering. It is an uneasy questioning as to whether death and suffering are real in Christianity. If there is a greater life that lives on both sides of death, I wonder, can death be real? And if the greater life is light, can suffering be real? I think of Aquinas saying Christ enjoyed the beatific vision of God all during his earthly existence and even during his passion and death.[12] I have always tended to reject that idea, thinking it takes away from the reality of Christ's suffering. How can joy coexist with sorrow? And yet the peace I am finding here in the Rothko Chapel does co-exist with the suffering and death I am facing in these dark stations of the cross. I can *feel* the reality of the joy! I can *see* the reality of the sorrow!

There are signs not only of life but of joy that subsists in the depths of sorrow, signs again of the standpoint I must take to enter into what is happening here, for I feel the peace while I am facing the suffering and death I see. What are the signs? Mark Rothko said of Milton Avery, "In a generation which felt that it could be heard only through clamor, force and a show of power" he "had that inner power in which gentleness and silence proved more audible and poignant."[13] So it is here. There are *signs of joy* in the midst of sorrow, not "clamor, force and a show of power" but "silence" and "gentleness" and "inner power." It is a joy veiled by sorrow. It is here somehow in the light I see. "The walls are in full brilliant light, or in half shade or in full shade," Le Corbusier says of light in architecture, "giving an effect of gaiety, serenity or sadness."[14] Here the somber colors, the red and the black, prevent any effect of "gaiety" even in the harsh light of noon, and in the softer light of evening there is both "serenity" and "sadness." When I conjoin seeing and feeling, I can discern all the signs, the "silence," the "gentleness," the "inner power."

But what of Rothko's suicide? I call to mind again my visit when I first saw these somber colors, when I thought I was seeing despair, when I wanted to get out as quickly as I could. Now, on the contrary, as I think of the peace I am feeling here, I can only say what Rothko himself said of Avery, "I grieve for the loss of this great man. I rejoice for what he has left us."[15] I form again my reply, to the child's question about the reality of Jesus on the cross, to my own question about the suicide of the artist, "Yes, the sorrow is real and so the joy is real." Joy and sorrow go together, it seems, real joy and real sorrow, for at the heart of joy as well as sorrow there is care. If I were literally carefree, if I cared for no one and nothing, I would be incapable of joy as well as sorrow. At the heart of the suffering of Jesus, at the heart of all suffering, there is care. If I can say "the life in him was light," I can say also "the light in him was love."

"We adore thee O Christ and we bless thee," I say once more, "because by thy holy cross thou hast redeemed the world," and I come full circle, back to the station where I began. I look again into the rectangle of black on the large field of maroon, and I take stock of what has been happening. I wonder if all I have been seeing and feeling in these stations is really there, or if I have only been going through a kind of Rorschach test where you are shown ten black or colored inkblot designs and asked to describe what they look like to you and so to reveal how intellectual and emotional factors are integrated in your perceptions. I do think it is at least a Rorschach experience I have been having and that it does indeed reveal how I conjoin seeing and feeling. I believe it is more, although I have not been trying to prove something so much as to come to an insight. These stations are occasions of insight for me, and the insight I come to is not into the paintings so much as into life and light and love. So I ask myself once more the child's question, "Was Jesus real when he was on the cross?" I am asking now, though, about the reality of what I am seeing and feeling.

As I gaze again at this station where I began, as I look again into this rectangle of black that I have taken to be the dark mirror of death, I seem to be looking into an empty tomb, like the disciples of Jesus on Easter morning when he had risen from the dead. "The result of my life is simply nothing, a mood, a single color," Kierkegaard says. "My result is like the painting of the artist who was to paint a picture of the Israelites crossing the Red Sea. To this end, he painted the whole wall red, explaining that the Israelites had already crossed over, and that the Egyptians were drowned."[16] That seems to be the result of my seeing and feeling, "simply nothing, a mood, a single color," as if Jesus had already gone through the suffering and death I have been facing, as if he were risen from the dead. And so he has, and so he is. It is "simply nothing, a mood, a single color," and yet it is a nothing that is no-thing, a mood that is a feeling of presence, a color that is a seeing of light.

There are *signs of reality* here in the midst of unreality. I think of a dialogue I have read, between Albert Einstein and Rabindranath Tagore, "On the Nature of Reality," that begins with Einstein asking "Do you believe in the Divine as isolated from the world?" and Tagore replying "Not isolated."[17] Signs of reality, as I am thinking of them, are signs of human reality, the reality of Jesus on the cross, yet not isolated from divine reality. What are the signs? These three that appear at first to be signs of unreality, "simply nothing, a mood, a single color." They become signs for me as I become aware of no-thing, of presence, of light. They are signs of human reality insofar as they mark the standpoint I must take to encounter them: the facing, the feeling, the seeing is human. They are signs of divine reality insofar as I encounter God in them: the no-thing, the presence, the light is divine. Still, it is not simply a matter of knowing but one of loving, for in knowing you are taking reality into yourself but in loving you are plunging into reality. You plunge in by way of willingness, "for without your will you were fashioned," as is said in the Talmud, "without your will you were born, without your will you live, without your will you die."[18]

At the beginning of his own *Stations of the Cross*, Barnett Newman, a fellow artist and friend of Rothko's, quotes these words from the Talmud, using the translation "against your will . . . " instead of "without your will . . . ,"[19] emphasizing the conflict of the human will with God and Jesus' sense of being abandoned, "My God, my God, why hast thou forsaken me?"[20] There is already an answer, no doubt, in the willingness of Jesus, "not as I will, but as thou wilt."[21] As I form my own reply again to the child's question about the reality of Jesus on the cross, though, I realize I am speaking also to this conflict of the human will, of my own will, with the reality of being fashioned and born, of living and dying, "Yes, the willingness is real and so the seeing and the feeling is real." I am trying to enter into the standpoint of Jesus facing death and suffering, I mean, and he becomes real for me, and what I am doing becomes real for me, if and when I become willing myself to face death and suffering.

I catch up with the reality that outruns necessity and possibility and impossibility and contingency, that is, when I become willing, when I say *yes* to having been fashioned and born, to living and to dying. The outrunning is the resurrection from the dead. Here is where the real difficulty has been for me, I believe, underlying my uneasiness about suffering and death in Christianity. It has been my unwillingness to face suffering and death myself. "Christianity 'outruns' the cross," the reality outruns the symbol, but I remain stranded at the symbol, or the cross remains for me "an unresolved symbol," until I become willing, until I embrace suffering and death. And yet now I do see and feel the reality that outruns the symbol. There is a reaching beyond the signs to the life, the joy, the reality they signify. It is perhaps what Roland Barthes calls "the imagination of the sign,"[22] the reaching of imagination from signifier to signified and to contrasting and related signifiers. I am hoping it is more, that I am going now from imagining to willing, that I am actually plunging into the life, the joy, the reality.

It is true, when Barthes says "Christianity 'outruns' the cross," he means only "there is a consciousness of a kind of vertical relation between the cross and Christianity: Christianity is under the cross as a profound mass of beliefs, values, practices, more or less disciplined on the level of its form."[23] For me the reality outrunning the symbol is the resurrection of Jesus, and my own catching up with the reality is my own entering into the resurrection, my own going through death to life, through suffering to joy. All the "beliefs, values, practices," I believe, are themselves "signifiers." All the signs of our times really are signs of a greater reality, a greater life that lives through death, a joy that is deeper than sorrow, a human reality that is not isolated from divine reality.

What then are the signs of our times? Christianity "presents salvation to human beings in a person rather than a doctrine,"[24] Pierre Rousselot says, meaning the person of Jesus Christ. So too, I will say, the signs of our times are persons, men and women who are signs of life in the midst of death, of joy in the midst of sorrow, of reality in the midst of unreality. Here signifiers and signified are one. As I go from station to station in the Rothko Chapel, I go from signifier to signifier. It is essential for me, though, to face the suffering and death I am seeing and feeling in these stations, and when I do face it myself I find the life that lives on through death, the joy that subsists in the depths of suffering. I enter into the reality of the signified, and so I myself become a sign in which signifier and signified are one. I enter into the person of Jesus Christ, he disappears from in front of me, as it were, and I find myself living the life, tasting the joy, plunging into the reality, as if it were my own. Is it really my own? That is a question that brings me back again to the child's question about the reality of Jesus.

"God goes to die tomorrow that you may possess him," Max Jacob says in the opening line of his poem "Way of the Cross."[25] Is God really my own? Is the life, the joy, the reality really my own? That is the question I have been asking, I think now, as I have been asking myself the child's question, "Was Jesus real when he was on the cross?" Each time I have asked I have answered "Yes," affirming the reality of the death he was facing, of the suffering he was undergoing, of what I myself was seeing and feeling as I entered into his standpoint. Each time too I have found something more, the reality of the life he was living, of the joy in the depths of his suffering, of the willingness I had to have to embrace life and death, to embrace joy and sorrow with him. Now I can see the reality is that of my own life and death, of my own joy and sorrow, of my own willingness. If I am real, he is real, and if he is real, I am real.

I come thus to an "I am," almost like that of Descartes, "I think, therefore I am," only the question is not simply skepticism but Docetism, a deeper skepticism, about being not simply about knowing. "If I am real, he is real," I say, passing over into the standpoint of Jesus, "and if he is real, I am real," I say, coming back again to myself. As willingness becomes love, I pass over, I plunge into being, by way of love ("I love our Lord Jesus Christ," Max Jacob says at the beginning of a meditation on the way of the cross),[26] and as consciousness becomes knowledge, I come back again to myself, I take being into myself, by way of knowledge. I begin to understand the mysticism of Paul the Apostle, "I have been crucified with Christ; it is no longer I who live, but Christ who lives in me."[27]

As I reflect on what I am saying about reality, though, and on what an imaginative thing I am doing, passing over into the standpoint of Jesus, seeing what he is seeing, feeling what he is feeling, I begin to realize the Docetism of our times is a separation of reality and imagination. To pass over I must put reality and imagination back together again. "If I am real, he is real," I say, and I begin to realize the enormity of what I am saying. For I am proposing to plunge into reality by way of love. It would be absurd to give my heart to something that is simply a matter of fact. It would be equally absurd to give my heart to something that is purely imaginary. Only "heart speaks to heart." It is in the person that reality and imagination are one. I pass over into someone rather than something. I embrace a Christianity that "presents salvation to human beings in a person rather than a doctrine," salvation because by passing over into the standpoint of Jesus, I believe, I come into a human reality that is no longer isolated from divine reality. There is a connection, I suspect, between the separation of reality and imagination in our times and the isolation of the human from the divine. It is this separation, this isolation, I think, that is the essence of "dark times."

I pass over into an "I am," therefore, where there is no isolation, no separation. "How powerful, even to being overpowering, and how legitimate, even to being self-evident, is the saying of *I* by Jesus!" Martin Buber says in *I and Thou*. "For it is the *I* of unconditional relation in which the man calls his *Thou* Father in such a way that he himself is simply Son, and nothing else but Son."[28] That is what I find in passing over into the standpoint of Jesus, "unconditional relation," a relation with God encompassing the whole human being, a relation that subsists even in "My God, my God, why has thou forsaken me?" ("If separation ever touches him," Buber says, "his solidarity of relation is the greater; he speaks to others only out of this solidarity.") I enter into his relation with God, and so when I come back again to myself, when I say "and if he is real, I am real," his relation becomes my relation with God. Again I begin to realize the enormity of what I am saying. Still, "*I* and *Thou* abide," Buber says; "everyone can say *Thou* and is then *I*." When I pass over and come back, I become a sign, and everyone becomes capable of being a sign to me, a child asking a question, for instance, a mother wondering.

I pass over by way of love, and I come back by way of knowledge. So it is "in a person rather than a doctrine" that I find Holy Wisdom. There is the figure of the woman playing before God in the beginning of time; there is the figure of the child playing at the end of time; and now there is the figure of the man calling out to God in the fullness of time. When I pass over, the figure disappears, and I find myself looking into the face of death and suffering, seeing what he is seeing, feeling what he is feeling. When I come back again to myself, I ask myself "And what do *you* see? What do *you* feel?" And I wait for my own heart to speak.

NOTES

1. Matthew 16:3 (from the King James Version, changing "ye" to "you").
2. Hannah Arendt, *Men in Dark Times* (New York and London: Harcourt Brace Jovanovich, 1968), p. ix (I have changed the indirect to direct discourse, leaving out "that" at the beginning and in the phrase "and that such . . .").
3. Shakespeare, *Macbeth*, Act V, scene 5, lines 26 to 28.
4. Roland Barthes, *Elements of Semiology*, trans. Annette Lavers and Colin Smith (New York: Hill & Wang, 1968), p. 38.
5. Philippians 4:7.
6. Diane Waldman, *Mark Rothko, 1903–1970: A Retrospective* (New York: Harry N. Abrams and Solomon R. Guggenheim Foundation, 1978), p. 68.
7. Exodus 20:4.
8. Rothko quoted by Clair Zamoiski in Waldman, *Mark Rothko*, p. 279.
9. Quoted by Dore Ashton, *About Rothko* (New York: Oxford University Press, 1983), p. 185.
10. John 1:4 ("In him was life, and the life was the light of men.").
11. Rainer Maria Rilke, *Selected Letters 1902–1926*, trans. R. F. C. Hull (London: Macmillan, 1946), p. 393 (Letter to Witold von Hulewicz, November 13, 1925). Cf. my discussion of this in *The Reasons of the Heart* (New York: Macmillan, 1978), pp. 88–91.
12. Cf. Aquinas, *Summa Theologiae*, III, q. 46, a. 8.
13. Mark Rothko, "Commemorative Essay" in Una E. Johnson, *Milton Avery* (Brooklyn, N.Y.: Brooklyn Museum, 1966), p. 15.
14. Le Corbusier (Charles Edouard Jeanneret-Gris), *Towards a New Architecture*, trans. Frederick Etchells (London: Architectural Press, 1952), p. 171.

15. Rothko in *Milton Avery*, p. 16.
16. Sören Kierkegaard, *Either/Or*, trans. David F. Swenson and Lillian Marvin (Garden City, N.Y.: Doubleday, 1959), p. 28 (Kierkegaard is speaking here with the voice of his Aesthetic Man). Waldman quotes this passage to illustrate Rothko's own work in *Mark Rothko*, p. 58.
17. Rabindranath Tagore, *The Religion of Man* (Boston: Beacon Press, 1961), Appendix II, "Note on the Nature of Reality" (conversation of Einstein and Tagore in the afternoon of July 14, 1930), p. 222.
18. *Aboth*, Chapter 4, Mishnah 22, trans. J. Israelstam, p. 57 in *The Babylonian Talmud*, vol. 8, ed. I. Epstein (London: Soncino Press, 1935). I have put "you" and "your" for "thou" and "thy," etc.
19. Barnett Newman, *The Stations of the Cross* (New York: Solomon R. Guggenheim Foundation, 1966), p. 9 (he has "Against thy will art thou formed . . ."). Newman's stations were done in the years 1958–1966, Rothko's in the years 1965–1966.
20. Matthew 27:46 (cf. Mark 15:34). Jesus is quoting Psalm 22:1. I keep the "thou" here and in the following quotation as in the Revised Standard Version to avoid confusion for the reader between the human "you" and the divine "thou."
21. Matthew 26:39 (cf. Mark 14:36 and Luke 22:42).
22. Cf. Barthes, "The Imagination of the Sign" in Susan Sontag (ed.), *A Barthes Reader* (New York: Hill & Wang, 1982), pp. 211–217.
23. Ibid., p. 213.
24. Pierre Rousselot, *L'intellectualisme de Saint Thomas* (Paris: G. Beauchesne, 1924), p. 109 (where in a passage that begins "*Mais le Christianisme . . .*" he speaks of "*le mystère de l'Incarnation, qui présente le salut aux hommes dans une personne plutôt que dans une doctrine*").
25. "*Dieu va mourir demain pour que tu le possèdes,*" opening line of the poem "*Chemin de croix,*" in Max Jacob, *L'homme de cristal* (Paris: Gallimard, 1967), p. 29.
26. Max Jacob, *La défense de Tartufe* (Paris: Gallimard, 1964), p. 231. Cf. my book *The Church of the Poor Devil* (New York: Macmillan, 1982), pp. 131–141 on consciousness becoming knowledge and willingness becoming love.
27. Galatians 2:20.
28. Martin Buber, *I and Thou*, trans. Ronald Gregor Smith (New York: Scribner's, 1958), pp. 66–67.

5. "The heart speaks"

on arriving at
a point of inflection

Whenever I don't know what to do, to say, to think, I ask myself what is on my heart. Nothing to do, nothing to say, nothing to think—it is then the heart speaks. It is under the sign of silence, of gentleness, of inner power, as I have found in Ayasofya, and among the giant redwoods, and now at the Rothko Chapel. I live in unconditional relation, nevertheless, where all is "I and thou," only in passing over and coming back, not simply in abiding in my own existence. As I have begun, so I will go on, passing over and coming back, until my heart speaks clearly at last.

To say "The heart speaks" is to say that in choosing what to do, what to say, and even what to think, I am guided by feeling, not by feeling alone, to be sure, but by feeling conjoined with seeing. Suppose I am at a loss. There is a way of seeing that is embodied in poetry, in the choosing of words, as I am doing now, and there is another way of seeing that is embodied in photography, in the choosing of viewpoints, as I was doing in Ayasofya and among the giant redwoods and at the Rothko Chapel, "two ways of seeing,"[1] as they have been called, but also of feeling, I will say, for I am guided by feeling in choosing words, in choosing viewpoints. If I am at a loss, it is not for words or for viewpoints but for some new awareness, some new realization. And now I have it—my heart has been speaking all along! What has my heart been saying? The answer is there for me in these "two ways of seeing," in my choosing of words, of viewpoints.

I have come to "a point of inflection," as it were, like one of the inflections of a river, where curvature changes, as seen on one side, from concave to convex, and as seen on the other, from convex to concave. For me the change is from inner to outer and from outer to inner. I have to turn the inside out, letting the heart speak clearly in my choice of words, and the outside in, going back from the eyes to the heart in my choice of viewpoints. I come upon "the imagination of the heart,"[2] as it is called in Genesis and Deuteronomy and Jeremiah and Luke, something that is prone to evil, according to these scriptures, and not simply an expression of the heart's desire for life and light and love. I come upon the darkness of the human heart, that is, as in the saying of Jesus, "from within, out of the heart of man, come evil thoughts, fornication, theft, murder, adultery, coveting, wickedness, deceit, licentiousness, envy, slander, pride, foolishness."[3] I realize my choosing of words, my choosing of viewpoints, has been a discerning between good and evil. I have been discerning between life and death, light and darkness, love and coldness.

Still, I believe there is a universal voice to be heard in discerning the good, and though "God is greater than our heart,"[4] God speaks to our discerning when the heart speaks. I have to work out "rules for the discernment of spirits,"[5] accordingly, rules for discerning good and evil in the promptings of the heart. Let me see if I can discover what rules, if any, I have actually been following, without fully realizing it, in choosing words, in choosing viewpoints, and so what my heart has actually been saying.

A WORD IN THE WORDS

Once when asked about his disciples, what they sought and found, Al-Alawi said "inward peace," but then some went further, he added, and found "self-realization in God."[6] These are what I have been seeking and finding, I believe, returning to my hill of dreams, coming into Ayasofya in Istanbul, starting on a wanderyear of soul, going from station to station in the Rothko Chapel. *What is inward peace*, I ask myself now, *and what is self-realization in God?* These two are the rules I have been following, I think, in choosing words, in choosing viewpoints, without having defined them in so many words or demonstrated them in so many views. Is it possible to define them by saying, to demonstrate them by showing, I wonder, or is the very choosing of words the saying, the very choosing of viewpoints the showing? It is in the very choosing, I expect, I will find the discerning of my heart's desire.

It has been said "the lover's discourse is today *of an extreme solitude*,"[7] as if the lover's choice of words were made by many but warranted by none. I have found myself speaking here again and again as a lover, saying "I have loved God more than I thought," taking to myself the words of the young woman, "You are in love with Ayasofya," marveling at the words about the child, "He had no smile, but the love in his large grey eyes was deep as the center," making my own the words of Max Jacob, "I love our Lord Jesus Christ." It is instructive to compare *A Lover's Discourse* written in our times by Roland Barthes and *The Book of the Lover and the Beloved* written centuries ago by Ramon Lull. Both are series of fragments, as if the lover's discourse were essentially fragmentary. Both are "of an extreme solitude." Both speak of the foolishness of love—Lull even calls himself "Fool of Love."[8] There is an irony here, nevertheless, at least for Lull whose discourse is of the love of God, for the fragments point to wholeness, the solitude to communion, the foolishness to wisdom.

If there is "an extreme solitude" in the discourse of the heart, as if the heart were speaking a private language, were saying things that are incommunicable, the solitude is nevertheless universal, is a wilderness where all human hearts are dwelling. Thus the utterances of the heart are communicable after all, from heart to heart in solitude. Here is the irony of the lover's discourse, and it is because of the irony, because of the wholeness, the communion, the wisdom, that I can look here for "inward peace," for "self-realization in God." As I choose words, as I choose viewpoints, I am actually moving from fragments to wholeness, from solitude to communion, from foolishness to wisdom. I am actually entering into "inward peace," actually undergoing "self-realization in God." I am moving toward a oneness where knowing and loving are one, where God the known and the loved is one, that is, and I the knower and the lover am thereby one, where I have invested all my knowing and my loving in God and I have invested all myself in knowing and loving. That oneness, I think, is "self-realization in God," but I have a foretaste of it in "inward peace."

Who is the lover? Who is the beloved? In Lull's fragments it is Ramon himself who is the lover and Christ who is the beloved. In my own sentences, as I look over them, I am the lover, I find, and God is the beloved; then Ayasofya is the beloved; then the Ancient Child is the lover; then Christ is the beloved. Yet I don't stay in my own seeing and feeling but am always seeing with the other's eyes, feeling with the other's heart. So in the end lover and beloved are one for me in knowing and in loving. As I speak of oneness, I think of Nikos Kazantzakis in his spiritual exercises, when he comes at last to oneness, saying "Even this One does not exist!"[9] What does the heart say, I wonder, of this One, of oneness in knowing and in loving?

It is after saying "Only you and I exist," then saying "You and I are One," that Kazantzakis ends up saying "Even this One does not exist!" These three sentences sum up a lover's discourse. It is different, though, addressing a lover's discourse to God, as he is doing, and addressing it to another human being. If I say "Only you and I exist" to another human being, I am plunging into "an extreme solitude" as if it were reality, a solitude where I am alone with you. When I go on to say then "You and I are One," I mean "You and I are alone," "alone" in the etymological meaning, "all one," but also in the meaning of its original usage, "all alone." It is not far from there to "I am alone," and that is what is meant, I think, when I say to another human being "Even this One does not exist!" I plunge into solitude with another, but I end up there alone—I think of loneliness, how much more acute it is for me after I have loved and lost another human being than it was before I had ever met the other, when I was alone and unaware of my aloneness.

If I say then to God, finding myself in this acute loneliness, "Only you and I exist," I come upon what I am calling "the darkness of the human heart," upon the good and the evil of my longing. For it is good to be with God and evil to exclude others. I think of Al-Hallaj, a great lover of God, who thought the sin of Satan, the primal sin, is jealous love, a love of God that wants to have God to oneself, a jealousy that "comes of loving a God whose love cannot be limited to one alone."[10] There is something very difficult here for a human lover. Lull speaks of "the secrets" of his beloved, and you can feel the ambiguity of his longing, to reveal the secrets and share God with others, his lifework and the point of his lover's discourse, and yet to keep the secrets and have God to himself, "for secretly the Lover hides the secrets of his Beloved, secretly also he reveals them, and yet when they are revealed he keeps them secret still."[11]

Love's secrets remain secret even when they are revealed, he is saying, God's secrets, that is, when we are speaking of the love of God. And so it is. I can speak of loving God, of loving Ayasofya, of loving Christ, and yet reveal no secret, for nothing I say will make sense except to another who loves. All one finds, without loving, are the fragments of discourse, the feeling of "an extreme solitude," the impression of foolishness or infatuation. It is only in loving that one finds wholeness, communion, wisdom in a lover's discourse. All the same, I feel uneasy when I speak of God, of Ayasofya, of Christ in terms of love. I want "the road of the union of love with God" to be a secret life, and I take comfort in the thought that love's secrets will remain secret from all but lovers, even if I reveal them. I think of Solovyov, describing his "three meetings" with the figure of Wisdom (whom I am calling Ayasofya, naming the person for the place) and saying to her, in front of others, at the beginning and again at the end of his poem, "Eternal friend, I shall not name you,"[12] as if naming her would reveal her, as if not naming her would keep her secret.

She remains secret, even if I reveal her, to one who sees only infatuation in a lover's discourse, only a foolishness that is the very opposite of wisdom, only a strong and unreasoning attachment to someone or something more imaginary than real. It is important to me, nevertheless, to reveal her, even if she remains secret, for if I can let go of jealousy, if I can let go of secrecy, I can love with an open heart, and if Al-Hallaj is right about the primal sin, I am uprooting in myself not only the root of hatred and "the crimes of passion" but also the root of coldness and "the crimes of logic"—jealousy is the root of that hatred and that coldness. Or then again, maybe *uprooting* is not the right word, since the root is really the heart's longing for God, however deviate it has become through jealousy, and I am not really uprooting it but letting go of God, letting God be God for everyone, letting the heart run its own true course.

"There are crimes of passion and crimes of logic,"[13] Albert Camus says. At the bottom of both of them, if I am on the right track, is a heart's longing that is good but that becomes evil by excluding others from its fulfillment. As I go back through the inflections of my own heart's longing, I begin to understand. There is feeling without seeing, as in "the crimes of passion," and there is seeing without feeling, as in "the crimes of logic," but when seeing and feeling are conjoined, when I am fully conscious, there is only one choice left to make and that is between a will and a willingness, a will to pursue my heart's desire and a willingness to follow my heart's desire. It is a subtle choice, as between a will to walk alone that excludes all companions and a willingness to walk alone that welcomes the companionship of others. It is a choice between keeping and sharing the secrets of the heart's desire. There is something in me that wants to keep them and something that wants to share them. "The secrets of love, unrevealed, cause anguish and grief," Lull says; "revelation of love brings fervor and fear." What is more, the secrets of the heart's desire are the secrets of God. "In the secrets of the Lover are revealed the secrets of the Beloved," he says, "and in the secrets of the Beloved are revealed the secrets of the Lover."[14]

What secrets? Secrets that are no secrets, that are no private matter, I mean, the secrets of a universal love, of "a God whose love cannot be limited to one alone," of a heart that longs, in spite of all jealousy, for a love that is universal. If I say then to God, "You and I are One," and I mean the universal love you are is my own true heart's desire, I come up directly against the choice I have to make between will and willingness. I can make one last effort to have God to myself by "willing despairingly," as Kierkegaard says, to be myself. His formula is a helpful one for me at this point, suggesting as it does that my desire to have God to myself is a desire to be myself and that the evil is not in being myself, not even in having God to myself, but in "willing despairingly," in taking something that can only be given as a gift. I think of a child just learning to talk, who has just learned the word *No* and who has learned at the very same time, as seems usually to happen, the word *mine*. My temptation is to say "No" to God the giver and "mine" to God the gift.

My alternative, I conclude, is to say "Yes" to God the giver and "yours" to God the gift. "No" and "mine" is the choice of will; "Yes" and "yours" is the choice of willingness. Actually I can see, as I formulate them in this way, there are not just two but four choices, three of them already formulated by Kierkegaard[15] and a fourth the one I am coming to here. There is first the choice of saying "No" to God the giver and "yours" to God the gift. It is the choice of unwillingness, a choice that is hidden in my feelings of being unloving, unloved, unlovely, when I seem to myself to be leading a life without love. Kierkegaard calls it "despair at not willing to be oneself." Then there is the choice of saying "No" to God the giver and "mine" to God the gift, the choice of will and of jealous love, my wanting to have God to myself, "the despair of willing despairingly to be onself." And then there is the choice of saying "Yes" to God the giver and "mine" to God the gift, a choice of will that is becoming willingness, a love of receiving but not yet of giving, where I receive myself from God as a gift, where by relating to myself and willing to be myself, according to Kierkegaard's formula, I am "grounded transparently" in God. Finally there is the choice I am coming to here, that of saying "Yes" to God the giver and "yours" to God the gift, the choice of willingness, of receiving that becomes giving, turning everything over to God, as in the words I have heard a friend use in prayer, "Everything is in your hands."

If the universal love that God is and the human heart's desire are one and the same, if they have one and the same object, that is, then my "Yes" to universal love is "Yes" to my own heart's desire, as if I were seeing with God's eyes and feeling with God's heart when I follow my heart's desire, and that is what it means to say "You and I are One." What is more, my "yours" to universal love is "mine" to heart's desire, as if to say what is yours is mine and what is mine is yours, and that is what I am saying or what I am enacting when I say "Everything is in your hands." So the feeling that is there in saying "mine" in a jealous love and also in a love that is only a receiving is not obliterated, and selfhood is not obliterated, in saying "Yes" and "yours."

A lover's discourse, Barthes says, "has no recourse but to

become the site, however exiguous, of an *affirmation*,"[16] an affirmation, he means, of love itself. My own discourse certainly has become the site of an affirmation, with my "Yes" and "yours." When he says it "has no recourse," he is suggesting there is no choice. I have been thinking of my affirmation, nevertheless, as a choice, setting it beside alternative choices, of a lovelessness, of a jealous love, of a love that is only a receiving and not also a giving. When he says "however exiguous," he seems to be thinking of a lover's discourse in comparison with other forms of discourse, how it is spoken by many but warranted by none. I think of that concluding sentence of Kazantzakis, "Even this One does not exist!" If I am really choosing, though, as I believe, choosing words at least and in choosing words choosing to love, to plunge into reality, then the site of my affirmation is not as exiguous as it first seems. I am choosing to love and to know, to pass over into the One, the unity of lover and beloved, and to come back again with new awareness to myself. When I pass over, I plunge into the reality of the One. When I come back again to myself, I come back to the reality of my own separate existence.

If I say then "Even this One does not exist," I mean the unity is in knowing and in loving and not in a state of existing. I mean "love is a direction," as Simone Weil says, "and not a state of soul," a direction that I find in the universe in passing over into union with God, that I find in my own heart in coming back to myself, and not a state of soul that takes away all passing over and coming back, that takes away all self between me and God. "It is only necessary to know that love is a direction and not a state of soul," she says. "If one is unaware of this, one falls into despair at the first onslaught of affliction."[17] For if I am hurled back upon myself by affliction, it can seem that union with God does not exist at all. When I pass over, though, and feel that encompassing peace I have felt again and again, I find it does exist as a direction in which I am facing, seeing with God's eyes, feeling with God's heart, and when I come back again to myself, I find it subsists as a direction in my own life, seeing with my own eyes, feeling with my own heart.

When I pass over, I can see the afflicted and I can feel their affliction. "We pass quite close to them without realizing it,"

Weil says. "What man is capable of discerning such souls unless Christ himself looks through his eyes?"[18] (I remember once seeing a blind man turned away at a bank teller's window, and I recall going, after I had obtained money at the window, to find him, walking in the direction I had seen him taking, looking for him and never finding him, looking at each person I passed on the streets, as if someone else were looking through my eyes, seeing each one as someone in need, as someone in affliction.) Yet I feel more and so I see more than affliction in the afflicted. I feel the joy of feeling with God's heart, of Christ himself looking through my eyes, the joy of union, the encompassing peace, and so I see the joy hidden in the affliction. When I come back to myself then, I find the joy in my own existence, even while I find also in myself the root of affliction, the loneliness of my separate existence. I find the joy even while seeing with my own eyes, even while feeling with my own heart, for I realize just as in passing over I am seeing what God is seeing and feeling what God is feeling, so in coming back God is seeing what I am seeing and feeling what I am feeling—the union is indissoluble as long as I abide in love.

I begin to understand the words "God is love, and he who abides in love abides in God, and God abides in him."[19] It is true, "only God is love right through,"[20] as More says to Norfolk, when they are speaking of human friendship and of the darkness and unreliability of the human heart. Still, the love that God is can be found as a direction that runs through the whole universe, that runs through the human heart in spite of all its darkness. So love is one, I conclude, much more truly one than it is many. We are caught up in love again and again in our lives without understanding what it is, missing the direction that is there in our hearts, and so we become like a diverging rather than a converging series, and love appears to be manifold rather than one. Yet all along there is really one direction, like time's arrow but without the compulsion of time, going always from the past into the future.

As I go from the past into the future, I am always waiting on God, always waiting for my heart to speak. I go into the morrow, but I am uncertain at times as to whether I am going under the inspiration of love or under the compulsion of time. God is "subtle," More says. There is such a thing as the dread of the morrow—I can feel it sometimes on a Sunday evening as I contemplate the week to come. When I go from the past into the future under the compulsion of time, I feel the dread of the morrow. When I go under the inspiration of love, I have a sense of being on a journey with God, a sense of adventure in going into the unknown. There is a desolation of the spirit that arises out of the compulsion of time, I can see, and a consolation of spirit that arises out of the inspiration of love. If "love is a direction," though, "and not a state of soul," I can be going in the direction of love and yet be feeling only the compulsion of time. Thus I wait on God. I wait for my heart to speak, "awaiting the word that will justify me."[21] Love's direction is like time's arrow, but feeling it is "inward peace," and the unity of love is like the unity of time in the universe, but feeling it is "self-realization in God."

Time's arrow is something we come upon in irreversible processes like aging and in our sense of time lapsing.[22] Leonardo da Vinci speaks of "the man who with perpetual longing looks forward with joy to each new spring and to each new summer, and to the new months and the new years, deeming that the things he longs for are too slow in coming; and he does not perceive that he is longing for his own destruction."[23] When I am unaware of life passing, of aging, of heading toward death, I am always longing for what is to come. When I do begin to realize our life is irreversible and the time of our life is lapsing, I begin to feel the dread of the morrow. When I become willing, however, when I say my "Yes" to God and my "yours" to the gift of life, time's arrow becomes love's direction for me, the "perpetual longing" becomes the love that comes from God and goes to God, the universal love that God is, and I am heading no longer toward my own destruction but toward the consummation of love in unity.

As time's arrow becomes love's direction, the unity of time in the universe becomes the unity of love, in our consciousness, I mean, and in our willingness. For Leonardo the longing for what is to come exists not only in the human soul but also in the universe at large, as a "quintessence," as "the spirit of the elements" that pervades the world, and so the human being is an image of the universe, "a type of the world." It is true, time's arrow from a scientific point of view is simply the direction from past to future we find in irreversible processes. There are elementary processes that are reversible ("according to our present knowledge," Einstein says, "all elementary processes are reversible"),[24] and so there is doubt as to whether time's forward direction holds always and everywhere. If we do feel the direction in ourselves as a longing, nevertheless, and do not separate seeing and feeling, we can see the quintessential longing, as Leonardo does, wherever we see the trace of time.

I come to a unity, therefore, when my own heartbeat is in unison, as it were, with the heartbeat of the world. It is a unity of direction, from past to future, felt as a longing that becomes love when I give myself over to it, a unity of knowing and of loving, of seeing with God's eyes and of feeling with God's heart. It is as if *One* were the first word as well as the first number, or better, the last word, as in an argument of lovers, for it is the Many who are the One, the "I and thou," as in the words of Jesus, "I and the Father are One."[25] If time is indeed "a changing image of eternity," this One is a unity into which I enter as time's arrow becomes longing in me, as longing becomes love. I am still troubled, though, by those words of Kazantzakis, "Even this One does not exist!" Does what I see when I conjoin seeing and feeling, does the unity I see really exist?

A VIEW IN THE VIEWPOINTS

"Subtle is the Lord God," Einstein says, "but not malicious."[26] It is a saying that speaks to doubts about order in the universe, doubts that came over theology in the fourteen century, that come over physics in the twentieth century. Einstein's theory of relativity has to do with the relativity of viewpoints, of observers in space and time, and so with God who is "subtle," but it calls for truths that hold true in every viewpoint, as in the ancient saying "universals are everywhere and always" (*universalia sunt ubique et semper*),[27] and so for a God who is "not malicious." As I reflect on the viewpoints I have been choosing, on what I see when I conjoin seeing and feeling, I wonder if the unity I see is analogous to the truths that hold true in every viewpoint, to the universals that are "everywhere and always." Or does the unity go deeper, does the conjoining of seeing and feeling carry me past the universal truths to the very God who is "subtle but not malicious," to a view in the viewpoints, to a unity with God in knowing and in loving?

I have not been separating the act of seeing and the act of knowing, seeing with my eyes, knowing with my mind. I can distinguish them, nevertheless, in terms of what is seen and what is known, like the visible and the invisible parts of a spectrum. I think of Plato's "divided line,"[28] the metaphor he uses of a continuous line divided into unequal portions according to the "golden section" so that the smaller is to the larger as the larger is to the whole. As I understand it, the visible is the smaller and the intelligible is the larger, for seeing reaches only to the visible but knowing reaches to the visible and the invisible. Seeing, I gather, can be pervaded by knowing, by a knowing that reaches beyond the limits of pure seeing. Something like this has been happening in all my seeing, I believe, as I conjoin seeing and feeling, seeing from my hill of dreams, seeing the light and feeling the peace in Ayasofya, finding a presence among the giant redwood trees, like Brother Lawrence seeing the tree in winter, seeing the suffering and death in the stations at the Rothko Chapel and finding there a peace that is veiled in the sorrow, seeing everywhere and always more than I can ever see with just the naked eye.

It is in a moment of shock, when something I was counting on is suddenly taken away from me, when the future I was looking forward to unexpectedly gives way to a very different prospect, when I can no longer seem to conjoin seeing and feeling but seem to myself to have gone blind and numb, it is then words like these speak to me, "Subtle is the Lord God, but not malicious." For they seem to say there is a meaning in what is happening, there is a future, and the golden proportion of seeing and knowing still holds. If there is an order in the universe, I expect it is this very thing, the "divided line," the "golden section," the golden proportion of the seen and the unseen. To say time is "a changing image of eternity" is to speak of this proportion, time belonging to the realm of the seen, eternity to that of the unseen, and the relation, "a changing image of," holding everywhere and always between the seen and the unseen.

I feel I am at the dividing point now, between the seen and the unseen, between seeing and knowing. I am feeling God's subtlety. "I find him rather too subtle . . .", More says. "I don't know where he is nor what he wants."[29] That is how I am feeling now, waiting on God, waiting for my heart to speak. I wonder if my heart will speak clearly if I move along the "divided line," from where I have been to where I am, starting with the visible, the realm of my seeing and my choosing of viewpoints, coming to the divide where I am now, then going on, if I can, to the invisible, the realm of the knowing in my seeing, to verify the unity I see.

There is always a choice in seeing, as in this riddle for children:

> Look in my face, I am somebody;
> Look in my back, I am nobody.[30]

Answer: A mirror. I am always looking in the mirror's face where there is somebody rather than in the mirror's back where there is nobody. That has been my choice in choosing viewpoints, looking from my hill of dreams, looking in Ayasofya, looking among the giant redwood trees, looking at the stations in Rothko. There is always somebody, myself, the woman playing before God in the beginning of time, the child playing at the end of time, the man calling out to God in the fullness of time. My seeing, I realize, has not been separated from my imagining. What would it be to look in the mirror's back? To see nothing from my hill of dreams but memories of the past superimposed on realities of the present, to see nothing in Ayasofya but a museum once a mosque once a church, to see nothing in the giant redwood trees but a stand of the oldest and tallest trees in the world, to see nothing in the stations at Rothko but abstract paintings in red and black. There would always be nobody, "nothing . . . but . . ."

I am seeing from different viewpoints, almost as in the principle of relativity, when I see somebody, when I see nobody in what I am seeing. What is more, I am interacting with what I am seeing, almost as in the uncertainty principle of physics, when I conjoin seeing and imagining. (I say "almost," speaking as I am in metaphor more than in principle.) I am seeing with "light-bearing eyes," as Plato says, and seeing becomes for me a two-way rather than simply a one-way process. "So I hold that the invisible powers of imagery in the eyes may project themselves to the object," Leonardo says, "as do the images of the object to the eyes."[31]

Is it only myself I see, then, as in a true mirror? No, I think it is more. It is possibility I see, when imagination comes into play. It is my own possibility, to be sure, but my possibility overlaps with possibility that is larger than myself. There is sometimes a unity, an encompassing peace, a well-being, sometimes a duality, seeing and feeling, light and presence, knowing and loving, and sometimes a trinity, mind and heart and soul, life and light and love. In each instance it is a possibility for me that is a possibility also for everyone. Here is where I come upon universal truths, possibilities that are possible for all human beings, "universals" therefore that are "everywhere and always." Indeed, the possibilities overlap with one another. When I conjoin the two of the duality, when I conjoin seeing and feeling, that is, they become a unity in knowing and in loving that is felt as a well-being, as an encompassing peace. When I consider the three of the trinity in relation to the two, the life and light and love in relation to the light and presence, they too coalesce into a unity, as in the command to love "with all your heart, and with all your soul, and with all your mind." I seem to be moving at last toward some one universal truth, like Eckhart saying "Existence is God" or Gandhi saying "Truth is God."

I come up short only when I remember again the feeling I have of God being "subtle." I see what I am seeing, I know, because I conjoin seeing and imagining. It is my approach that decides what I can see, almost as in Einstein's saying "it is the theory which decides what can be observed."[32] If I approach the mirror from the front, I see somebody, but if I approach it from behind, I see nobody. Still, there is truly somebody to see in the mirror's face, just as there is nobody to see in the mirror's back. God too is seen and unseen, seen as a possibility larger than myself when I join seeing and imagining together, unseen when I put them asunder. I have to discover God then not in

seeing alone, not in imagining alone, but in the knowing that
pervades seeing and imagining, the knowing that knows to join
them together, that knows to discern possibility and to recognize possibility that is greater than myself.

Here I come upon the divide between the seen and the unseen, between seeing and knowing. It is like the continental
divide where all streams on one side flow east and all those on
the other flow west. Yet seeing and knowing are also the current
and the undercurrent of one and the same stream of consciousness when seeing is pervaded by knowing. What is seeing? What
is knowing? There is a clue, I think, in the way Plato divides his
line between the visible and the intelligible, especially if he
divides it, as I think, according to the "golden section" where
the smaller part is an image of the larger (i.e., the smaller is to
the larger as the larger is to the whole). I take this to mean
seeing is an image of knowing and the seen is an image of the
known. If this is the order there is in the universe, and all we
can see is an image of all we can know, then the seen is an
ongoing revelation of the unseen, and time is "a changing image
of eternity." Where then is the subtlety of God I have been
feeling? Here it is: The unseen is also the unknown. It becomes
known only as eternity is revealed in time, only as I come to
insight into image.

If I say of God "I find him rather too sutble . . .", as More
does, and "I don't know where he is nor what he wants," I am
speaking out of an encounter with the unseen in my seeing,
with the unknown in my knowing. It takes the form of an
encounter with the unexpected in my life when I had expected
a greater continuity between past and future, between retrospect, that is, and prospect. I didn't expect "a changing image
of eternity" to change as much as it actually does. So now, as I
wait on God, as I wait for my heart to speak, I don't know what
to expect.

"At the frontier of the unheard-of—"[33] Dag Hammarskjold
writes in his diary, speaking of a border like this, between the
seen and the unseen, between the heard-of, as he calls it, and
the unheard-of. As long as I remain at this divide, waiting on
God, waiting to see, that is, and waiting for my heart to speak,
waiting to hear, I am like Dag before he said his "Thanks!" for

the past, before he said his "Yes!" to the future. It is as if I had not fully said my own "Yes" to God and my own "yours" of the gift of life, though I have been talking about saying it. For a certain kind of order has broken down for me, one according to which I can confidently answer "Yes" to the question "Will the future be like the past?" To say "Yes" to the future, as Dag does, without being able to answer "Yes" to that question about the continuity of the future with the past, requires a more outright reliance on God, a more absolute "Yes" to God, a more thoroughgoing "yours" of the gift of life than I had been envisioning. I am being asked to enter into "unconditional relation" with God. So my heart *is* speaking clearly at last!

I have been waiting to see, waiting to hear. Now I see the possibility, I hear the call of "unconditional relation" in a way I did not as long as I was assuming the future would be like the past. It is a seeing pervaded by knowing, a hearing pervaded by understanding. It is true, I don't have to enter into such a relation with God merely to answer the question "Will the future be like the past?" There is a continuum of possible answers, it has been said, ranging all the way from utter uniformity of past and future, through various degrees of partial uniformity, to a limit situation where anything can happen.[34] If I cross over now to the other side of the "divided line," if I pass over into the knowing in my own seeing, into the understanding in my own hearing, it is not simply to find the answer. It is to realize the difference between counting on time and counting on eternity in time, between relying on the past and relying on God.

"The 'unheard-of'—to be in the hands of God,"[35] Dag says after saying "Thanks!" and "Yes!" That is what it is for me too, after saying "Yes" and "yours," "to be in the hands of God." There is a knowing in this, a knowing of the unseen, of eternity in time, and there is an understanding, an understanding of what it is to be in the hands of God, of what it is to rely on God. I do find in my knowing, as I pass over into it, an answer to the question I have been asking about the continuity of the future with the past. There is a continuity, I find, not of the future with the past so much as of eternity in time. If I run the gamut of possible answers, from perfect uniformity of past and future, through all the degrees of imperfect uniformity, to no uniformity where anything can happen, I do not come across this answer, for in all of those answers there is an assumption that order is uniformity and if there is no uniformity, there is no order in the universe. What I have come upon is order of another kind, a continuity indeed but a continuity of eternity in time rather than of time with time. It is order where anything can happen, where God is "subtle," but where I can rely on God, where God is "not malicious."

I know, when Einstein says "Subtle is the Lord God, but not malicious," he may well mean, as he often used to say, "God does not play dice,"[36] expressing his misgivings about statistical interpretations of physical events, at least about taking statistics as the last word. There is a connection, nevertheless, with what I am talking about here, as I go from relying on the past to relying on God. As long as I am relying on a continuity of the future with the past, I am indeed relying on a probability, as in a dice game, and when I go from that to relying on God, I am assuming "God does not play dice." If we look at what God is doing simply in terms of time, comparing past and future, retrospect and prospect, then it can seem God does play dice, I want to say, but if we look at it in terms of eternity in time, thinking of time as "a changing image of eternity," then it seems clear God does not play dice.

"Everything that exists is situated," Max Jacob says in the preface to *The Dice Cup*, his book of prose poems. "Everything that's above matter is situated; matter itself is situated."[37] I too am situated, I am situated in place and in time, and so I cannot avoid the perspective of time, and thus of the dice game (Max's "dice cup"), I gather from this, even if I look at time in terms of eternity. It is like the riddle of the mirror: Look time in the face, and you can discern the face of eternity; look time in the back, and you can discern nothing but time. I choose to look time in the face, but I cannot forget or ignore what it is to look time in the back. Memory, understanding, will: I cannot forget, I cannot ignore, but I can choose. Thus looking time in the back, I find myself saying of the order we live in, "It is order where anything can happen," but looking time in the face, I find myself saying it is order "where I can rely on God." I do choose, moreover, or I am always choosing, again and again, to rely on God, and out of this choosing and this relying and this being in the hands of God, there comes an understanding.

What understanding? It is a wisdom that comes with the simplicity of relying on God. There is a wisdom that comes with the passage of time, that comes of looking time in the back, of relying on the continuity of the future with the past, that comes of surprise when fears prove groundless, of disappointment when hopes prove vain—it is the wisdom that comes as one hardens one's heart because of sorrow and loss, that means self-defense in a difficult world. There is another wisdom, and this is the one I am speaking of now, that comes with awareness of eternity in time, that comes of looking time in the face, of turning everything over to God, where surprise and disappointment at the unexpected yield to wonder at the unknown—it is the wisdom of remaining God's child in trust and obedience, of knowing what is "enough for me," as in Newman's prayer "one step enough for me" or in Loyola's "Give me thy love and thy grace, for this is enough for me."[38]

Let me divide the "divided line" again, this time my own way rather than Plato's, letting the continuous line be the stream of consciousness, both the current of seeing and the undercurrent of knowing. I am wading up the stream, as it were. What is behind, flowing away from me, is the past, all I have seen and known; what is ahead, flowing toward me, is the future, all I have yet to see and know; and where I am, the point of division, the "golden section" itself, is the present, all I now see and know. There is a unity now of time and eternity: seeing is pervaded by knowing and time is pervaded by eternity. Since I am dividing according to the "golden section," moreover, the past is an image of the future. Thus there is a continuity of past and future after all, a continuity really of eternity in time. So I am in a very simple and obvious place, in the present with the past behind me and the future ahead of me, a place where "one step" is indeed "enough for me" and where to take that step "thy love and thy grace" are indeed "enough for me." There are two elements here, "style or will and situation or emotion,"[39] as Max Jacob says, "style or will" in my relation to past and present and future, my "Yes" and "yours," "situation or emotion" in the relation of past and present and future to me, God calling, the heart speaking.

Now I understanding what it is "to be in the hands of God." It is this double relation, this to and fro, on the one side the relation of past and present and future to me, the encompassing peace I have felt again and again, that becomes *inward peace* as it enters my heart and soul, and on the other my own relation to past and present and future, my response to the peace of God, that becomes *self-realization in God* in my "Yes" and "yours." The unity I see when I conjoin seeing and feeling is in this double relation, and it exists as truly as the relation exists. As I stand in the present with the past behind me and the future ahead of me, I can feel time's arrow as a longing, and I can see it as the tangent of a great circle of love that comes from God and goes to God. "Unconditional relation" means being heart and soul in the longing, and my heart's speaking is calling me ever more fully into the great circle of love.

Here at the point where time's arrow is tangent to the great circle of love, there is union with God, a unity with God in knowing and in loving. It helps me to envision union with God in this way, with this image of being "tangent," touching, that is, time's arrow in my life touching the great circle of love, the present moment being the point that is common to time's arrow and eternity's circle. It is a unity but not a simple equating of God and human being, although the circle rolls along the arrow and the unity holds at every point in human existence, at every present moment in a life. Time and eternity remain distinct while touching at every point in time. My "I am" and the great "I am" of Exodus and John's Gospel remain distinct while touching at every point in the story of my life. Thus I feel time's arrow as an unfulfilled longing, but every time I become conscious of touching ("inward peace") and willing to touch ("self-realization in God"), the longing becomes the love that comes from God and goes to God, the great circle an old man of the desert described to T. E. Lawrence in the words, "The love is from God and of god and towards God."[40]

I have meditated on these words before, and as I let them speak to me now, I think of a friend who wrote me lately saying these words hold among human beings, that the love between one human being and another is "from God and of God and towards God." If that is true, then the great circle of love does indeed pass into the stream of time. It enters time in this present moment between us. We can stop the flow, nevertheless, by our fear of one another. "I saw an image of a single person," my friend wrote, "and an image of myself standing next to that person—and there was a barrier to the flow of love between us because of fears on my part that inhibited the flow." If I let go of fear, then "the love I share with others comes from God," she said *through* the other, to me, and then flows back." If I stop the flow out of fear, then I feel only the longing, but if I let go of fear (love "casts out fear"),⁴¹ then I feel the love.

At the point of inflection where I am now in the stream of time, I have been letting my heart speak in my choice of words and I have been going back from my eyes to my heart in my choice of viewpoints. Have my choices inhibited the flow of love or have they let the love come through? Here is my ultimate rule for discerning good and evil in the promptings of the heart, the rule by which I may judge the rules I have been following in choosing words, in choosing viewpoints, "inward peace" and "self-realization in God." I realize now in retrospect how the love has been coming from God, through others, to me—through a friend saying of the giant redwood trees "It was very healing to be near them and in the forest" and "The fatigue of the days dropped from us and we were small creatures again in a big world made by God"; through a young Turkish woman saying "You are in love with Ayasofya" and telling me "Turn to life, God is in your heart!"; through a child asking "Why doesn't God feed the poor people?" and "Was Jesus real when he was on the cross?"; through a friend praying "Everything is in your hands!"; and now through a friend saying this very thing, "the love I share with others comes from God, through the other, to me, and then flows back." It has indeed been coming from God, through the other, to me. Does it then flow back?

Yes, its coming to me takes the form of an encompassing peace that becomes "inward peace." Its flowing back takes the form of my "Yes" and "yours" that becomes "self-realization in God." There are three rules, I could say, spelling it out, for discerning the good in the promptings of the heart, analogous to the three rules Wallace Stevens gives for "a supreme fiction":

> It must be abstract;
> It must change;
> It must give pleasure.[42]

I seek a supreme reality rather than "a supreme fiction," a reality that is "from God and of God and towards God," and so I say it is

> a way for everyone,
> leading beyond expectation,
> bring peace of heart and soul.

It is the fulfillment of universal human longing, I mean, and so it is a possibility for everyone and not for myself alone. It is not simply the longing itself, though, but the love, and so it is always unexpected in the course of human events. Still, it is the fulfillment of longing, and so it gives peace of heart and soul.

How can I tell a supreme reality from "a supreme fiction"? I think of a Platonic love that rises from passion for the individual to ecstasy in contemplation of the ideal—it is the ideal that would be "a supreme fiction." Saying this, however, depends on separating reality and imagination, on relegating the individual to reality and the ideal to imagination ("By supreme fiction, of course, I mean poetry,"[43] Stevens says.) If we put reality and imagination back together again, we can trace not only the rising movement of longing but also the flow of love coming to us and going from us. It is the longing ("love" in Plato's dialogues) that rises from passion to ecstasy. It is the love ("love" in the New Testament) that comes from God and goes to God. The love is a true human experience, is as real as the longing, is not just the ideal of longing but its real fulfillment. So reality is not just the individual devoid of possibility, not just time devoid of the unexpected, nor is peace of heart and soul just imagination devoid of reality. Instead the "really real" turns out to be "from God and of God and towards God."

It is when the heart speaks that I encounter the "really real." I find it first in the form of longing with its direction in time, from past to future, then in the form of love with its direction in eternity, from God to God. It is in this direction where time's arrow touches eternity's circle, where "from past to future" becomes "from God to God," that I find the good in the promptings of the heart, that I find unity with God in knowing and in loving. When I find a direction that is a possibility not only for me but for everyone, that goes beyond my expectations of a future that is like the past, that brings peace of heart and soul even in the midst of affliction, then I know I have found my way.

NOTES

1. Wilson G. Pinney, *Two Ways of Seeing* (Boston: Little, Brown, 1971).
2. Genesis 6:5 and 8:21 (both in King James and in Revised Standard Version); Deuteronomy 29:19 and 31:21 (in King James only); Jeremiah 3:17, 7:24, 9:14, 11:8, 13:10, 16:12, 18:12, 23:17 (in King James only; Revised Standard Version has "the stubbornness of the heart" and the like in these places); Luke 1:51 ("he has scattered the proud in the imagination of their hearts"; both in King James and in Revised Standard Version). 1 Chronicles 29:18 (King James), however, uses it in a positive sense ("O Lord God of Abraham, Isaac, and of Israel, our fathers, keep this forever in the imagination of the thoughts of the heart of thy people, and prepare their heart unto thee.").
3. Mark 7:21–22 (cf. Matthew 15:19).
4. 1 John 3:20.
5. Cf. "Rules for the Discernment of Spirits" in *The Text of the Spiritual Exercises of St. Ignatius*, trans. John Morris (Westminster, M.D.: Newman, 1943), pp. 106–114.
6. Cf. Martin Lings, *A Sufi Saint of the Twentieth Century* (London: Allen & Unwin, 1971), pp. 21f.
7. Roland Barthes, *A Lover's Discourse*, trans. Richard Howard (New York: Hill & Wang, 1978), p. 1.
8. Ramon Lull, *The Book of the Lover and the Beloved*, trans. E. Allison Peers (London: Society for Promoting Christian Knowledge, 1923), p. 25.
9. Nikos Kazantzakis, *The Saviors of God: Spiritual Exercises*, trans. Kimon Friar (New York: Simon & Schuster, 1960), p. 131.
10. Herbert Mason, *The Death of Al-Hallaj* (Notre Dame, Ind.: University of Notre Dame Press, 1979), p. 30.
11. Lull, *The Book of the Lover and the Beloved*, pp. 38–39.
12. Vladimir Solovyov, "Three Meetings," trans. Ralph Koprince, in Carl and Ellendea Proffer (eds.), *The Silver Age of Russian Culture* (Ann Arbor, Mich.: Ardis, 1975), pp. 128, 134.
13. Albert Camus, *The Rebel*, trans. Anthony Bower (New York: Knopf, 1967), p. 3.
14. Lull, *The Book of the Lover and the Beloved*, p. 39 (#76) (cf. p. 29, #31), and p. 56 (#155).
15. All these formulas are in Sören Kierkegaard, *Sickness unto Death* (pub-

lished with *Fear and Trembling*), trans. Walter Lowrie (Princeton, N.J.: Princeton University Press, 1968), p. 182 ("despair at not willing to be oneself"); p. 200 ("the despair of willing despairingly to be oneself"); and p. 147 ("by relating to itself and by willing to be itself the self is grounded transparently in the Power which posited it"—Kierkegaard's formula for faith, the state in which there is no despair).

16. Barthes, *A Lover's Discourse*, p. 1.
17. Simone Weil, *Waiting for God*, trans. Emma Craufurd (New York: Putnam, 1951), p. 135.
18. Ibid, p. 119.
19. 1 John 4:16.
20. Robert Bolt, *A Man for All Seasons* (New York: Vintage, 1962), p. 70.
21. Psalm 119:123, as translated in *The Liturgy of the Hours* (New York: Catholic Book Publishing Co., 1975), 3:940 (in the versicle and response, "My eyes keep watch for your saving help.—Awaiting the word that will justify me.").
22. The phrase "time's arrow" is Sir Arthur Eddington's in *The Nature of the Physical World* (New York: Macmillan, 1929), p. 69. Cf. the use of the phrase more recently in the realm of biology, Harold F. Blum, *Time's Arrow and Evolution* (Princeton, N.J.: Princeton University Press, 1968), and in the realm of chemistry, Ilya Prigogine and Isabelle Stengers, *Order out of Chaos* (New York: Bantam, 1984), pp. 257–289.
23. Irma A. Richter (ed.), *Selections from the Notebooks of Leonardo da Vinci* (New York: Oxford University Press, 1952), p. 276.
24. Albert Einstein, "Reply to Criticism," in Paul Arthur Schilpp (ed.), *Albert Einstein: Philosopher-Scientist* (Evanston, Ill.: Library of Living Philosophers, 1949), p. 688.
25. John 10:30.
26. *Raffiniert ist der Herr Gott, aber boshaft ist er nicht*, quoted by Margaret Shields in Schilpp, *Albert Einstein*, p. 691, and by Abraham Pais for the title of his biography of Einstein, *'Subtle is the Lord . . .'* (New York: Oxford University Press, 1982), p. vi.
27. Aquinas, *Summa Theologiae*, I, q. 46, a. 2.
28. Plato, *Republic*, VI, 509d–511e in *The Collected Dialogues*, ed. Edith Hamilton and Huntington Cairns (Princeton, N.J.: Princeton University Press, 1973), pp. 745–747. I am assuming the division is according to the "golden section." Plato says only the line is "divided into two unequal sections." He goes on then to subdivide "in the same ratio." I am ignoring here the subdivisions and considering only the division into the seen and the unseen.
29. Bolt, *A Man for All Seasons*, p. 38.
30. Monika Beisner, *Monika Beisner's Book of Riddles* (New York: Farrar, Straus & Giroux, 1983), riddle 83.
31. Richter, *Notebooks of Leonardo da Vinci*, p. 112 (the idea is developed on pp. 112–118). Plato, *Timaeus*, 45; "light-bearing eyes" is mentioned in Richter's footnote on p. 116. Jowett translates "eyes to give light" in Hamilton and Cairns, *The Collected Dialogues*, p. 1173.
32. Einstein in conversation, quoted by Werner Heisenberg in his "Remarks on the Origin of the Relations of Uncertainty," in William C. Price and Seymour S. Chissick (eds.), *Uncertainty Principle and Foundations of Quantum Mechanics* (New York: Wiley, 1977), p. 5. It is the thought that led Heisenberg, according to his account here, to discover the uncertainty

principle. It seems remarkable to me that both Einstein's principle of relativity and Heisenberg's uncertainty principle have their origin in this same idea, that "it is the theory which decides what can be observed." According to the principle of relativity, if two physical systems are in relative motion, it is not possible to observe their motion with respect to an aether at absolute rest but only their motion relative to one another. According to the uncertainty principle, if a particle is in motion, it is not possible to observe at the same time its exact motion and its exact position. So both principles have to do with what can and cannot be observed, and both, though principles, are inferences from existing theory.

33. Dag Hammarskjold, *Markings*, trans. Leif Sjöberg and W. H. Auden (New York: Knopf, 1964), pp. 76, 80, 82.

34. Cf. Rudolf Carnap, *The Continuum of Inductive Methods* (Chicago: University of Chicago Press, 1952). Cf. especially his discussion of "uniformity" and "degrees of order," p. 66. On the question "Will the future be like the past?" see my discussion in *A Search for God in Time and Memory* (New York: Macmillan, 1969), pp. 3–4.

35. Hammarskjold, *Markings*, p. 100. Cf. also what he says about "the unheard-of" on pp. 96 and 101. All these entries in his diary come after the "Thanks!" and "Yes!" on p. 89, while those cited above in note 33 come before.

36. Cf. Pais, '*Subtle is the Lord* . . .', pp. 440 and 443.

37. Max Jacob, *The Dice Cup*, ed. Michael Brownstein (New York: SUN, 1979), p. 5.

38. See Newman's "Lead, Kindly Light" in *A Newman Reader*, ed. Francis X. Connelly (Garden City, N.J.: Image, 1964), p. 74, and Loyola's *Suscipe* ("Take, O Lord, and receive all my liberty . . .") in Morris, *The Text of the Spiritual Exercises of St. Ignatius*, p. 75.

39. Jacob, *The Dice Cup*, p. 7.

40. T. E. Lawrence, *Seven Pillars of Wisdom* (Harmondsworth, England: Penguin & Jonathan Cape, 1971), p. 364. See my discussion of this in *The Reasons of the Heart* (New York: Macmillan, 1978), pp. 1–3.

41. 1 John 4:18.

42. Wallace Stevens, "Notes Toward a Supreme Fiction" in *Collected Poems* (New York: Knopf, 1961), pp. 380, 389, and 398. (These three sentences are the titles of the three parts of the poem.)

43. He says this in a letter to the Cummington Press (May 14, 1942) in *Letters of Wallace Stevens*, ed. Holly Stevens (New York: Knopf, 1977), p. 407. But then in a letter to Henry Church (December 8, 1942) he says, "I have no idea of the form that a supreme fiction would take. The Notes start out with the idea that it would not take any form: that it would be abstract. Of course, in the long run, poetry would be the supreme fiction; the essence of poetry is change and the essence of change is that it gives pleasure"; ibid., p. 430. Then again cf. pp. 435, 438, 485. Also pp. 863–864 where he thinks of adding "It must be human."

6. "There is a way"

on sitting in the
Meditation Room at the UN

A way for everyone, leading beyond expectation, bringing peace of heart and soul—is there a way in a nuclear age? Living in our time, when life is threatened by nuclear death and destruction, must be like living in the time of the plague in the fourteenth century, when life was threatened by the Black Death. Then the very relation of human beings to life and death was changing, and now it is changing again and in the same direction, as it seems, from living toward life to living toward death. How to find once more a way of living toward life?

It is not a matter of life and death, I want to say, so much as a matter of our relation to life and to death. "They asked me what I thought of the atomic bomb," Gertrude Stein says. "I said I had not been able to take any interest in it."[1] If it is only a matter of life and death, I think she is saying, then there is no heart of the matter. As it is, we don't just live and die but we have always a relation to our life and to our death. I wonder, though, if there is anything I can do about life and death or even about our relation to life and death as I sit here thinking in the Meditation Room at the United Nations. If there is, it will not be something such as nations and peoples can do by working together. As I came in here one day, I saw a demonstration going on across the street with the large banner reading "Free Afghanistan." If there is something I can do, it will not be to set a people free. It will be rather to find a way of living and dying free, a way of seeing, of feeling, of living in God.

If I can find a way, if I can say "There is a way," I have done something. There is madness, seeing separated from feeling, in our use of the power of life and death over one another, and there is terror and despair, feeling separated from seeing, in our bowing down before that power as if it were sovereign in the universe. To say "There is a way" is to say that we can live free toward life and death by conjoining seeing and feeling, "heart-free" I will say, with heart in our seeing and freedom in our feeling, heart rather than madness, freedom rather than terror and despair. Master Eckhart's word for this is *Gelassenheit,* "letting be."[2] It is a word that can be used, as he used it himself, to mean a way of relating to the things of life, letting go of them and turning them over to God, or, as Martin Heidegger has used it in our times, to mean a way of relating to the things of modern technology, using them and letting them go, without any reference to God. I want to use the word as Eckhart himself did, and I want to use my own word *heart-free,* spelling it out in terms of "heart's ease" and "heart's longing," to mean a freedom toward life and death that comes of being in a relation to God. I want to say, like Eckhart saying "Existence is God," the wonder of existence is greater than the dread and fascination of death and, like Gandhi saying "Truth is God," the force of truth is greater than the force of arms.

It is essential "to pit meditative thinking decisively against merely calculative thinking,"[3] as Heidegger says, if we are to pit the wonder of existence against the dread and fascination of death, and it is essential to act, I think, upon the insight that arises in meditative thinking, if we are to pit the force of truth against the force of arms and of nuclear arms. Let me see if I can do all this in my own way, if I can pit the way of seeing I have learned against the madness, the way of feeling against the terror, the way of living against the despair of a nuclear age.

MIND'S EYE: A WAY TO SEEING

"It is for those who come here to fill the void with what they find in their center of stillness," Dag Hammarskjold says of the quiet and simplicity of the Meditation Room at the United Nations. I think of the Prayer of Quiet, as the mystics call it, and the Prayer of Simplicity. As I understand it, the Prayer of Quiet is the encompassing peace I have been finding, and the Prayer of Simplicity is the presence of God I have been learning to practice. *What do I find in my center of stillness?* If I ask myself that question, as Hammarskjold suggests, my initial answer is this quiet and simplicity. As I reflect further, though, I realize there is a way of seeing that arises out of the quiet and simplicity, a way I shall now call "mind's eye," using a phrase that goes back to Middle English, *myndes ye*, and that occurs also in Shakespeare, as when Horatio says "A mote it is to trouble the mind's eye" and when Hamlet says "Methinks I see my father"—"Where, my lord?"—"In my mind's eye, Horatio."[5] It is an expression that is often used to mean simply "an imaginary or a recollected sight, as opposed to one actually seen." I shall use it to mean a way of seeing in which outer vision is conjoined with inner vision, seeing with contemplation.

I wonder about the seeing that created the nuclear age. Can this same seeing be used to see beyond it? Or is an entirely other seeing required? According to Heidegger, it is "calculative thinking" (*rechnendes Denken*) that has created the age we live in, and it is "meditative thinking" (*besinnliches Denken*) that will take us beyond. "To be, or not to be, that is the question"[6] for us as for Hamlet; meditation is thinking about meaning, that is, and ultimately about the meaning of being. If "to be" has a meaning, as Heidegger believed,[7] a meaning that is one and not just many, as he learned to believe from studying Duns Scotus, then there is indeed a question as to what the meaning is, a question that is felt in the very wonder of existence, the wonder that anything exists at all and not rather nothing, and there is a choice to be made, the choice "To be, or not to be."

"It is not *how* the world is, that is the mystical," Ludwig Wittgenstein says, "but *that* it is."[8] It is not *how* things are, that is the wonder of existence, I want to say too, but *that* they are. Thus the meaning of the verb "to be" is both one and many, one when we are speaking of "the mystical," of the wonder of existence, and many when we are speaking of how things are, of the many modes of existence in the world. So too there is meditative or intuitive thinking that dwells upon "the mystical," upon the wonder of existence, and there is calculative or discursive thinking that goes from one thing to another, figuring out how things are. It is calculative thinking that has created the age we are living in, though not without the help of meditative thinking and the intuitive leaps that have occurred in physics and chemistry and medicine and related fields of learning in our time. And it is meditative thinking, seeing conjoined with contemplation, sight pervaded with insight, that promises to see beyond our situation, to see through the threat of death and destruction to the wonder of existence, to see clearly the choice that existence poses to us.

As I sit here thinking about thinking, about calculative and meditative thinking, I call to mind the phrase "thinking about the unthinkable,"[9] used some years ago to describe thinking about nuclear destruction, calculative thinking that envisioned possible nuclear wars and calculated the death and destruction they would entail. Let me see what would happen if I were to engage in meditative thinking about "To be, or not to be," if I were to pit a *memento mori*, a "remember to die," against the "forget to die" of one who calculates death, if I were to go from memory to understanding to will.

Two visions come to mind as I sit here in the twilight of the Meditation Room, one the creative radiance Vladimir Solovyov saw in the desert of Egypt when Holy Wisdom revealed herself to him, "like the first radiance of a universal and creative day," the other the destructive radiance people saw in the desert of New Mexico when the first atomic explosion occurred, "brighter than a thousand suns."[10] I don't see the "golden azure" of creation except in my mind's eye, but I do feel the wonder of existence. I don't see the sudden glare of destruction either except in my mind's eye, but I do feel the dread and fascination of death. These are my own real memories, the wonder of existence I have felt ever since childhood when I lay on my back looking up into a starry night and the dread and fascination I have felt ever since my late twenties when I saw my youth passing and my life opening up before me all the way to death. Our "to be" is in the wonder, our "not to be" in the dread and fascination. My own "to be" is in the wonder too, the awe of "I am," and my own "not to be" is in the dread and fascination, the awe of "I will die."

All I see with my eyes here is the twilight of this room, not the brilliance of a vision, either creative or destructive, and in the twilight I see a block of iron ore that has been set in the middle of the room, the ground, as it were, rising up from the ground, and beyond that a colored fresco that has been mounted in the front of the room, the focus, as it were, standing out from the focus. A ray of light falls upon the surface of the stone from above. Another illumines the colors of the fresco from below, the blue and the gray, the brown and the yellow. There is an emphasis here that hints of a vision yet to be. I am here on a "vision quest," I begin to realize, like a young American Indian keeping solitary vigil, or like a young Russian mystic, like Solovyov, traveling over land and sea to meet Holy Wisdom. I am waiting, I think, for the ground to become the ground, the focus to become the focus. I am waiting again for a conjoining, for seeing and feeling to come together into a unifying vision.

What is the ground? There is a clue in those words, "It is not *how* the world is, that is the mystical, but *that* it is." It is "mystical," I take it, that is the ground, the wonder of existence, the wonder that the world is, the wonder even that I am. The dread and fascination of death belongs, it seems, to how the world is, to how I am. Death is not the same as nonexistence; my dying does not make it as if I had never been. So the dread and fascination of death is not on a par with the wonder of existence. I think of the attempt to destroy evil in the world, or what we take to be evil, like Ahab harpooning Moby Dick in Melville's story, trying to remove evil from the world, but being caught in the toils of his own line as Moby Dick sounds and being jerked "voicelessly"[11] into the sea, killed in the act of killing. We cannot make evil as if it had never been, I gather, and we cannot ourselves be made as if we had never been. There is no annihilating of the wonder of existence. There is only killing and dying, only the changing of how we are and how the world is. Here is ground, a place to stand. Here is memory too, even if we forget.

What then is the focus? "The view (the seeing) of the world *sub specie aeterni* is the view of it as a limited whole," Wittgenstein goes on to say. "The feel (the feeling) of the world as a limited whole is the mystical."[12] If I bring seeing and feeling into focus with one another, as when I lay on my back looking up into the starry night, letting my feeling for the world be affected by my seeing and my seeing by my feeling, I see and feel the world "as a limited whole." To see it *sub specie aeterni,* "under the aspect of eternity," is to see it in terms of the wonder of existence; to feel it "as a limited whole" is to feel it as what is as opposed to what is not. Here is the focus of seeing and feeling. Here is the figure emerging from the ground of existence. I think of the figure of Wisdom, of Solovyov's vision, of his feeling "The infinite fit within its dimensions," of his seeing "What is, what was, and what will always be."[13]

As I reflect on the figure of Wisdom and on Solovyov's vision, I ask myself if I dare invoke her as he did and ask her to reveal herself to me. Does it make sense to invoke her, to actually speak to Wisdom? Jesus himself speaks of her and speaks of her speaking, "Therefore also the Wisdom of God said . . ."[14] It is not far from there to the thought of actually speaking to her. I think of the words of an antiphon I found in a Book of Hours:

> Wisdom of God,
> Be with me,
> Always at work in me.[15]

I say these words here in the Meditation Room, repeating them silently like a mantra whenever my thoughts wander. Meanwhile I meditate on the words of Solovyov, describing his vision, "What is, what was, and what will always be," and I hope the Wisdom of God will be with me, at work in me, as I meditate, and her presence, however subtle, will be my vision. I think of the Standing Silence in Tolkien's story when, before eating, people stand facing the sunset in a moment of silence, looking to the realm "that was" and beyond to the realm "that is" and beyond that to the realm that "will ever be."[16] That is what I am doing here, it seems, sitting rather than standing in silence.

I seem to be joining now the peoples who used to pray facing the sunset, whose great symbol was an altar at the crossroads (This block of iron ore in front of me is the altar, and the United Nations is the crossroads.), just as in Ayasofya I seemed to be joining the peoples who used to pray facing the sunrise, whose great symbol was a cave. I think of these people now, of all who have been forgotten, how most human beings who have ever lived have been forgotten and only a few have been remembered. This is "what was." It is a *memento mori*—"Tell me, where all past years are."[17] I sit here thinking of those who have been forgotten, almost like Augustine remembering forgetfulness. "Yet, however it may be, and in whatever inexplicable and incomprehensible way it happens," he says, "I am certain that I remember forgetfulness, even though forgetfulness obliterates all that we remember."[18] I search in human memory and I come to its limits in forgetfulness. I search for God in my memory and I find myself in God's memory.

Obliteration gives way to memory, I mean, because there is a God, because God "is not God of the dead, but of the living," as Jesus argues with the Sadducees, because "all live to him."[19] I am on the verge of an insight here, I can feel, like Eckhart's "Existence is God" and Gandhi's "Truth is God." There is a hint of it in Kierkegaard's remark "I every day ascertained and convinced myself anew that a God exists."[20] Every day I have been coming here to the Meditation Room; every day I have to ask a guard to unlock the room for me (The Meditation Room is kept locked!); every day then I enter into this twilight and sit here for several hours. Have I been ascertaining and convincing myself anew "that a God exists"? Certainly for me, God is "what is." To say "a God exists," for me, is to say also "all live to him." It is to say no one and nothing goes lost. So if I say "God is what is," I am saying something as sweeping as "Existence is God" and "Truth is God." It is the wonder of existence, that the world is, that I am, that makes me realize "a God exists," but it is this meditation on death I am doing now, this realizing death does not make us as if we had never existed, that "all live to him," that makes me realize God is "what is."

I don't mean God is everyone and everything. I mean rather everyone lives to God and everything exists in God. Here is "what will always be." Yet am I actually conscious of living to God? I am indeed alive and alive to God, but to be consciously so, that is eternal life! It is an encompassing, I expect, this existing in God, an encompassing peace as I have found in Ayasofya and in Rothko, an encompassing goodness and mercy. There is a suggestion of something like that here too, on a metal plague just inside the glass doors as you enter. It reads

> This is a room devoted
> to peace

and those who are
giving their lives
for peace.
It is a room of
quiet where only
thoughts should speak.

My thoughts are speaking, perhaps too much, but I can actually feel an encompassing peace here too, even at the United Nations, a surrounding quiet and simplicity that suggests the quiet and simple figure of Wisdom, that points the way to "peace on earth."[21] So I am conscious, even here, of existing in God.

As soon as I say "peace on earth," however, I think of the possibility of vision giving way to disillusionment at the presence of evil on earth. I think first of Hammarskjold himself, whose words are on the metal plague and who is largely responsible for the Meditation Room as it now exists with the block of iron ore in the middle like an altar. I think of a conversation he had in the last summer of his life with Bo Beskow, the artist who did the fresco on cement in the front of the room. "Do you still have faith in man?" Beskow asked. "No, I never thought it possible," he answered, "but lately I have come to understand that there are really evil persons—evil right through—only evil."[22] I think of Solovyov too, how he changed from the time of his youth when he wrote the poem "Three Meetings," describing his visions of the figure of Wisdom, to the time in his forties, in the last year of his life in fact, when he wrote the book *Three Conversations*, posing the question "Is evil only a natural defect, an imperfection disappearing of itself with the growth of good, or is it a real power, possessing our world by means of temptations, so that for fighting it successfully assistance must be found in another sphere of being?"[23]

There is something here that has to do with aging, with going from youth to age, from "your young men shall see visions" to "your old men shall dream dreams."[24] There is an element of experience with life in the awareness of evil and of its presence in human beings, something of a wisdom that comes with age. Yet there is something also of "dreams" in the wisdom of age, even of nightmares, just as there is something of "visions" in meeting the figure of Wisdom. Solovyov saw the danger here, the temptation of disillusionment, as he wrote in his own last years of the "tragedy,"[25] as he called it, of Plato's last years, of Plato going from the visions of his early dialogues to the dreams of his late dialogues, and especially the nightmares of his *Laws*, where laws are set down that would have justified the condemnation of Socrates. There is a temptation we all face, I gather, in passing from youth to age, to give way to disillusionment, to let the figure of Wisdom be replaced by the wisdom of age.

What of evil then and its presence in human beings? Thinking about thinking and about "mind's eye," as I am doing here, I think of the words of the Sermon on the Mount, "The eye is the lamp of the body. So if your eye is sound, your whole body will be full of light; but if your eye is not sound, your whole body will be full of darkness."[26] The King James Version has the more literal translation, "single" for "sound" and "evil" for "not sound." The meaning is not an "evil eye" as in folklore, I believe, an eye whose glance is harmful, but it may well be more than just an impaired sight as the translation "not sound." It may be an eye that is "evil" as in the parable of the generous householder and the laborer who grumbles about others receiving as much pay as he, "Or is your eye evil because I am good?"[27] It may be envy, that is, and hatred of the good. This is the primary evil, I have been learning, a turning of the heart's longing to envy and jealousy, wanting to have happiness to oneself, even to have God to oneself like Al-Hallaj's Satan, or if one is unhappy, wanting no one else to be happy. It is a turning of the heart's longing that clouds the mind's eye.

Still, there is a paradox here that can elude the wisdom of age, the wisdom that comes of meeting evil in oneself and in others in the course of experience. It is that good is at the heart of evil, that the heart's longing is at the "heart of darkness."[28] It is true, the heart is numbed in turning from the good for everyone to the good for oneself alone and, having found misery, to the good for no one, seeking company in misery, and what impresses you in meeting the numbed heart is just this, its "spiritual numbness," like the ice at the bottom of Dante's hell. You encounter the heart of darkness, the heart of ice, and you feel like Hammarskjold, "I have come to understand that there are really evil persons—evil right through—only evil," not fully realizing there is a heart in that darkness, a heart in that ice. You see the destructive power of the heart of darkness, the heart of ice, and you feel like Solovyov that evil is "a real power," not fully realizing its power is only in terror and despair.

Wisdom that goes beyond that of age, the Wisdom of God, I mean, has to be in the knowing of hearts, the heart of light and the heart of darkness, the heart of fire and the heart of ice. I think of Al-Hallaj, who was known as *hallaj al-asrar*, "the carder of consciences" or "the reader of hearts," and something Louis Massignon said of him after devoting a lifetime to studying his life, his influence, his teaching. "I do not pretend that the study of his life has yielded to me the secret of his heart," Massignon said, "but rather it is he who has fathomed mine and who fathoms it still."[29] I know what he means. I spend my time trying to fathom hearts, passing over to others and coming back again to myself, but it is my own heart that is fathomed and is being fathomed still. Just now, for instance, I have been speaking of the wonder of existence being greater than the dread and fascination of death. That is an attempt to fathom hearts, their wonder, their dread and fascination, but it is my own feeling for existence that comes to light, my own feeling for death. What is more, I find existence greater than death in an experience of existing in God, of being encompassed by God. That is my own heart being fathomed by the Wisdom that is greater than my own, an experience of being known and being loved.

Although I know of the heart's longing and I know it is at the heart of light and of darkness and I know it is a longing for God, I cannot fathom it, for I cannot penetrate its secret without penetrating God's secret. I cannot fathom the human heart without fathoming God. Still, I can feel my own heart being fathomed, I can feel myself being encompassed by God, being loved by God. A "cloud of unknowing" comes between me and God, as is said in *The Cloud of Unknowing*, not "that kind of darkness or cloud you can picture in your mind's eye in the height of summer, just as in the depth of a winter's night you can picture a clear and shining light," but rather something unfathomable, "for you cannot see it with your inward eye," and yet "The eye with which I see God is the same eye with which God sees me,"[30] as Eckhart says, for I can feel my heart being fathomed, and I can come to a knowing out of the experience of being known.

Here is my vision of the figure of Wisdom, an experience of being known and being loved, of someone "who has fathomed" my heart "and who fathoms it still." It is not the terrible knowing that comes of being caught up in the dread and fascination of death, an X-ray vision, as it were, of human skeletons. It is rather a healing sense of being known and being loved that comes of being caught up in the wonder of existence, not "I think, therefore I am" so much as "I am, therefore I am known and I am loved." I have to work at discerning my being known and loved from the ins and outs of my standing with other human beings, though it is true I come to this sense in passing over to others and entering into human standpoints and humanly designed situations as well as in simply being in the world and encountering the wonders of the universe. I have to differentiate the human experience of a divine fathoming from human failure, I mean, my own and that of others, to penetrate the secret of the human heart. When I become caught up in those ins and outs, in that human failure, I become caught up in the darkness of my own heart, in the unknowing that pervades my heart's longing. Then it is that I can mistake the darkness for the light and think that I have penetrated the secret and that it is terror and despair.

"If then the light in you is darkness, how great is the darkness!"[31] When I have been caught up for some time in the darkness of my own heart, unable to see in my mind's eye, to remember, to imagine the wonder of existence, I find help in some human token of being known and being loved, and I find healing in the assurance that there is someone, even the Wisdom of God, "who has fathomed" my heart "and who fathoms it still," albeit the heart has not yielded its secret to me. There is peace in being understood. What is more, there is understanding, a knowing that comes of being known, a loving that comes of being loved, that may yield the secret after all.

HEART'S EASE: A WAY TO FEELING

If I say of another human being, as Massignon does of Al-Hallaj, "it is he who has fathomed" the secret of my heart "and who fathoms it still," I am finding in the other an embodiment of the Wisdom of God. In fact, Al-Hallaj said of himself "I am the truth," and this, above all, is the saying that led to his trial and his execution. I think of Jesus saying "I am the way, and the truth, and the life," and also of Massignon dedicating his work on Al-Hallaj "to Jesus of Nazareth, crucified, King of the Jews."[32] There is a question of truth here and of true love. There is a truth that emerges in the human experience of being known and being loved. It is the truth of a heart that is restless until it rests in the understanding that comes of being understood, a truth that comes to light only in rest. I shall call that rest "heart's ease," using again a phrase that goes back to Middle English, *herts ese*, and that occurs also in Shakespeare, as when the Capulet servant Peter cries "Musicians, O musicians, 'Heart's ease, Heart's ease:' O, an you will have me live, play 'Heart's ease.' " "Why 'Heart's ease'?" they ask. "O, musicians," he cries, "because my heart itself plays 'My heart is full of woe.' "[33]

There is motion and there is rest in the realm of the heart, motion in the heart's longing, rest in the heart's ease. It is in motion that the heart itself plays the song "My heart is full of woe," in unrequited longing as when Henry V says "What infinite heart's ease must kings neglect, that private men enjoy," or when Caesar says of Cassius "Such men as he be never at heart's ease whiles they behold a greater than themselves." I think of the loneliness that is the mark of living in our time, that is so often expressed in diaries and autobiographies of the nineteenth and twentieth centuries, in Hammarskjold's diary, for instance, where "loneliness" is the most frequent word. "I heard the scream, the scream of terror, the voice of loneliness screaming for love,"[34] he writes just after the time when he spoke of "really evil persons—evil right through—only evil." I think also of Kafka writing in his diary, "There is no one here who has an understanding for me in full. To have even one who had this understanding, for instance a woman, would be to have support

from every side. It would be to have God."[35] There is an unrequited longing in this loneliness to be known and to be loved, a
longing for someone who fathoms the secret of one's heart. To
find such a one, "for instance a woman," I can see now, would
be to find a human embodiment of the Wisdom of God, for it
would be to "have support from every side," "to have God."

When I do actually find someone "who has an understanding
for me in full," I find it is not a reflective and highly conscious
understanding so much as an intuitive and indeliberate understanding that comes out in spontaneous and even inspired words
and gestures. When my heart plays "My heart is full of woe,"
when I am neglecting "infinite heart's ease" that others enjoy,
when I can "be never at heart's ease" for seeing others greater
than myself, someone who loves me, whose reflective understanding of me may indeed stop at what is wrong with me, can
reach beyond woe and neglect and envy with loving and a
spontaneous knowing that comes of loving, can touch the loneliness that lies under all with a heart's ease that I can never
contrive for myself. I sometimes think the Wisdom of God is
actually speaking to me through someone who loves and who
knows like this, someone who knows and can speak to the
longing of my heart, who knows also the darkness of my heart
but with a knowing that comes of loving. That must be it, a
knowing that comes of loving, that makes a human being an
embodiment of the Wisdom of God, that allows Wisdom to
speak through a human being.

What then of a saying like "I am the truth"? It is an "ecstatic
cry," as Massignon says, a spontaneous expression fo a knowing
that comes of loving. It answers, I believe, that other cry, "the
scream" that Hammarskjold speaks of, "the scream of terror,
the voice of loneliness screaming for love." I seem to hear both
the one cry and the other here in the silence of the Meditation
Room, the one calling, the other answering. There is truly infinite heart's ease in differentiating the sense of being known and
being loved that is of God, even though it comes through human beings, from the uncertainty of being known and being
loved that evokes the "scream," the "terror," the "loneliness."
Let me see if I can differentiate, if I can pass over into a
knowing that comes of loving, and then if I can integrate, if I

can come back again with that new sense to my own heart's longing.

Why was Al-Hallaj put to death? Why was Jesus put to death? Why is there such fear of a knowing that comes of loving? "Therefore also the Wisdom of God said 'I will send them prophets and apostles,' " Jesus quotes, " 'some of whom they will kill and persecute.' "[36] There is nothing we desire more, it seems, than to be known and to be loved, and yet there is also nothing we fear more. To pass over into a knowing that comes of loving, I can see, I will have to get past my fear. Or better, if I do pass over, I will leave my fear behind. There is fear of love and fear of death, as if to be known and to be loved were to die, to become an object, a naked body, a dead body. There is a fear of being uncovered, a fear of apocalypse, of revelation, of the X-ray vision of human skeletons. Here is the terror of our times and the basis of terrorism, the Red Terror of reovlution, the White Terror of reaction. It is shame at our nakedness, at our sexuality, at our mortality. If we do not pass over, we turn the subject, the one who knows and who loves, into an object, like Al-Hallaj on the gibbet, like Jesus on the cross, so that we will not be turned into objects ourselves. If we do pass over, on the other hand, if we do enter ourselves into the knowing that comes of loving, we become "heart-free," not just in the ordinary way of the phrase, "not in love," that is, and therefore free for love, but in a deeper way, free for love and free for death.

"I am not so much afraid of death, as ashamed thereof,"[37] Sir Thomas Browne writes in his *Religio Medici*. Here is the essence of my fear, not fear so much as shame, shame at the heart of fear. Here is my clue also to the knowing that comes of loving. There is a knowing that goes with shame, like Adam and Eve "knowing good and evil" and feeling shame at their nakedness. It is, I believe, a knowing that is unloving. Thus the shame at being known in this way. It is like being the object of an "evil eye." If the primal sin, that of Satan, has to do with loving, with a loving that is unloving, with jealousy, wanting to have God to oneself, then the original sin, that of Adam and Eve, has to do with knowing, with a knowing that is unloving, with envy, wanting to "be like God, knowing good and evil."[38] I have to pass, accordingly, from a sense of shame and of being known in this way without love, not really God's way who "sees like an enemy but is a friend,"[39] to a sense of being known and being loved, and so to a loving that is knowing and a knowing that is loving.

Is it a knowing that simply coexists with loving, as the phrasing "sees like an enemy but is a friend" can suggest, or is it a knowing that actually comes of loving? When I meet it in another human being, when I find someone who seems to fathom my heart, I feel no "in spite of," as if I were loved in spite of being known. Instead I feel known with a knowing that is loving, loved with a loving that is knowing. It is true, I also encounter a loving that reaches beyond knowing, and that most of the time, as I feel loved but not fully known. It is only at certain moments, in flashes of insight, that one who always loves me seems also for an instant to know me and to speak to my heart as if knowing the very secret of my heart. How can I tell, who do not know the secret myself? What would it be to fathom a heart? What would it be to fathom my own in its being fathomed by another, even by God? I think of Al-Hallaj when he was praying, the night before his execution, saying over and over again "illusion . . . illusion" until the night was almost over, and then, as dawn approached, suddenly crying out "truth . . . truth."[40] When I cannot seem to make the step from being known to knowing, I have a feeling of illusion, as if I were not really known and loved. When I begin to make the step, I have a feeling of truth.

Here is the turning point I am looking for in passing over, this point where I go from the feeling of "illusion . . . illusion" to the feeling of "truth . . . truth." What is the illusion? What is the truth? For Al-Hallaj both the illusion and the truth seem to be expressed in that fateful saying of his "I am the truth" (Ana'l-Haqq), the illusion in appropriating to himself the truth that God is, the truth in recognizing the truth of God dwelling within him. It is an "ecstatic cry" that becomes "illusion" when the ecstasy has gone out of it, that becomes "truth" again when it expresses the exalted state of feeling that cuts through our usual feeling of aloneness and separation from God and from one another. Somehow the "I am" of ecstasy that takes us beyond ourselves and our aloneness is in being known and in being loved, and "the truth" of ecstasy is in knowing and in loving. I know who am known. I love whom am loved.

"I am," as in Exodus and in John's Gospel, is an expression of the wild glory of God, the Shekinah of Jewish tradition, who fills human beings with the wonder of existence, and when she enters them, fills them with the wonder of their own existence. I think of a conversation I once had with David Daube on the "I am" sayings of Jesus where David maintained that is saying "I am," Jesus was not asserting himself so much as confronting others with the Shekinah, with the glory.[41] I think too of Eckhart saying whatever God gave to Christ he gave also to us, "he gave the whole to me, just as he did to him"[42]—a daring assertion, an "ecstatic cry," an "illusion" when the ecstasy has gone out of it and it becomes merely self-assertion, and yet a "truth," even "the truth," when it is spoken in the ecstasy of being known and loved, of knowing and loving. Ecstasy, nevertheless, is not an uncommon experience. It is the feeling of exaltation, of being carried beyond self-consciousness and loneliness by being known and being loved, self-consciousness giving way to the consciousness of being known, loneliness giving way to the consciousness of being loved. It is the passing of heart's longing into heart's ease. It is as common as moments of insight, as moments of being known and being loved, common but not commonly recognized.

What then of the uniqueness of Jesus? However common the experience of being known and loved, of knowing and loving, there is still the uniqueness of who is known and loved, of who knows and loves. The "who" and the "I am" are linked. I think of a conversation with Erik Erikson on the "I" of Jesus where he maintained the "I" is both universal and personal.[43] Jesus is speaking to the heart when he says "I," and so the "I" is universal, and he is speaking from the heart, and so the "I" is personal. As I understand it, according to my own faith in Jesus, I am invited to step into the place where Jesus stands, entering into his relation with God. Al-Hallaj too, if I understand him rightly, saw himself entering into Jesus' relation with God, modeling his life on the story of Jesus as it is told in the Koran.[44] "I do not pretend that the study of his life has yielded me the secret of his heart," I have to say now of Jesus as Massignon says of Al-Hallaj, "but rather it is he who has fathomed mine and who fathoms it still."

Yet I can discern a call to understanding in this, a call to pass over from my own heart being fathomed to the secrets of the heart that fathoms mine. It is as if the Lord in whom I believe wished to reveal his heart to me, to speak to me apart from the clamor of the many voices of other people, even though those voices too speak of knowing and loving. I have an image of us going aside, as it were, to speak heart to heart. I seem to be enacting that thought as I come in from the noise of the streets of New York and enter into the silence of the Meditation Room. I have a feeling of being singled out in this, of being known and loved and being called into knowing and loving, although I believe everyone else is singled out in the same way. It is a feeling that is reinforced as I ask the guard each day to unlock the Meditation Room for me, although the room is really meant for everyone. I come in here alone each time, although as soon as I am here other people always come in too, one by one, some staying for a long, some for a shorter time. I have the feeling of coming in from noise to quiet, from complexity to simplicity, the feeling of being freed from the many demands that make themselves felt in the many voices of my life and my times, the feeling of going from the many to the one, of coming to live in quiet and in simplicity.

I am still at a loss to fathom the secret of the heart that fathoms mine, unless it is an insight to realize that the love I am encountering here is a love that is personal and yet universal, like the "I" of Jesus, a love that singles me out and yet the love of one whose love cannot be limited to me alone. It is a love that is personal and yet transcendent, like the "I am" of Jesus, a love that flows into me and yet a love that I cannot contain, cannot hold on to, but must allow to flow on through me, that comes from God and goes to God. It is a love that comes and goes beyond the jealous love of Satan and the envious love of Adam and Eve. Perhaps the secret is in Al-Hallaj's cry of ecstasy, "I am the truth," if I may interpret those words to mean the truth for me is an "I" that is personal to one, to Jesus, and yet universal in all, an "I am" therefore that is personal to each one of us, even to me, and yet transcendent of us all. If the secret is in the sense of "I," if it is in the wild glory of "I am," then the heart of knowing and of loving is in being.

Of course I can also say it the other way around, the heart of being is in knowing and in loving. "I am, therefore I am known and I am loved," I can say, and "I know and I love, therefore I am." Saying it in this way goes beyond Descartes saying "I think, therefore I am," though it falls short of Al-Hallaj saying "I am the truth." Going beyond Descartes, nevertheless, and the "I am" that expresses only self-consciousness, it speaks to the fear and the shame of death, to the terror of our times that is bound up somehow with self-consciousness and loneliness. Consider the four forms of mystical prayer: quiet, simplicity, union, ecstasy. If knowing means taking reality into oneself, as I have been assuming, and loving means going out of oneself to reality, then quiet and union are to be found primarily in knowing, and simplicity and ecstasy are to be found primarily in loving. My starting point here in the Meditation Room has been quiet and simplicity. I have been letting myself be carried from quiet toward union, from simplicity toward ecstasy. Indeed I have been experiencing quiet and simplicity, union and ecstasy in their more subtle and more common forms, while falling short of the more intense and more rare forms that mystics describe. I am sitting here trying to discern what is subtle, making much of what is common. All the same, I am being carried beyond fear and shame, beyond terror.

"Human kind cannot bear very much reality,"[45] T. S. Eliot has the thrush say, speaking of the human encounter with eternity in time. So it is in the human encounter with knowing and with loving. I love the quiet, the simplicity. I can feel the quiet deepening into something that may be union, the simplicity intensifying into something that may be ecstasy. I begin to understand what it means to say love "casts out fear," and yet I cannot seem to stay here very long just rejoicing in being known and being loved. I can feel the ease of heart's ease, but I can also feel the unease of heart's longing. I am so used to living in the unfulfillment of desire, I guess, that I cannot bear the reality of fulfillment. I cannot stay here in the Meditation Room for more than two or three hours at a time without wanting to get up and go out again onto the streets of New York. Maybe what I really want is to go from being known to knowing, from being loved to loving.

"Quick," the thrush says, enjoy being known and being loved

while you can. "Go," it says then, learn to know from being known, learn to love from being loved. Maybe God wants to see with my eyes and to feel with my heart, as Max Jacob says in a witty prose poem called "Cosmogony":

God views the earth (there is a God) through the hoops of a barrel! He will see it like some teeth that are decaying. My eye is God! My eye is God! The decaying teeth have like a drop, infinitely tiny, that classifies them. My heart is God's barrel! My heart is the barrel! The universe for me is like it is for God.[46]

God is looking into a dice cup, the barrel, and he sees the dice that have hollow marks on them, like decaying teeth, each mark like an infinitely tiny drop. It is a cubist image, one image turning into another. Eye and heart are there, nevertheless, seeing and feeling, knowing and loving. As I understand it, "My eye is God!" means I know from being known by God, and "My heart is God's barrel!" means I love from being loved by God. I use God's knowing of me to know the universe. I use God's loving of me to love the earth.

To know with God's knowing of me, who "sees like an enemy but is a friend," is to know about the dice, to know about the decaying teeth, and to love with God's loving of me is to love human beings in their vulnerability to hap and mishap, to love them in their liability to death and decay. Al-Hallaj's ecstatic cry, "I am the truth," corresponds to Max Jacob's witty exclamations, "My eye is God!" and "My heart is God's barrel!" It is not that the dice, the hap and the mishap, or the decaying teeth, the death and decay, is "the truth." It is rather the knowing from being known, the loving from being loved. Ultimately it is the knowing that comes of loving. My eye is the lens, my heart is the barrel of a telescope that takes in the whole universe. I stand in the focus of knowing and loving, the place where Jesus stands in relation to God, and in that focus "The universe for me is like it is for God."

An ecstatic cry! A witty exclamation! All I really see and feel is the wonder of existence. Still, if I combine the wonder of existence with the dread and fascination of death, both very real to me, I do see and feel something like Max's "Cosmogony." My eyes now are like the lenses and my feeling for existence and my feeling for death are like the barrels of binoculars. I am bringing into focus the two visions with which I began, "I am" and "I will die." As I recollect my own past experience, I realize the first vision, that of the wonder of existence, came for me with an awakening of mind, while the second, that of the dread and fascination of death, came later with an awakening of heart. Love causes the awakening of heart, it seems, for most people; death did it for me, though it left me vulnerable to love. Yet there was feeling, I realize now, even in the first awakening, that of mind, a feeling of wonder that has never faded for me. As I bring the two forms of feeling together now, and the two forms of seeing, I think I am beginning to see and feel my way through the darkness I have always found lurking outside the circle of light, the darkness of the human heart.

If shame and the knowing of good and evil are at the heart of darkness, as I have been learning, then the darkness is not an unknown so much as a knowing that is unloving. It is true, a knowing that is unloving is also unknowing, is a knowing that is lacking in understanding. It is one thing to encounter the dread and fascination of death, to feel the shame. It is another to be caught up, to succumb. An encounter leaves room for other feeling, even for the wonder of existence. If I let my feeling of shame be pervaded by my feeling of wonder, I come to a sense of being known and loved, and I become capable of knowing and loving in my turn. If I feel wonder and shame but have not yet allowed shame to be pervaded by wonder, I am like the man Rilke describes at the end of his *Notebooks*:

What did they know of him? He was now terribly difficult to love, and he felt that One alone was able for the task. But He was not yet willing.[47]

That is what happens to me when I get caught up in the darkness of my own heart. "What do others know of me?" I ask myself. "I am now terribly difficult to love," I tell myself, "and only God is able to love me without distortion, but God is not yet willing." In reality it is I who am not yet willing to let myself be known and be loved. Letting the feeling of shame be pervaded by the feeling of wonder is a gradual process of opening the soul, of becoming willing. The sense of "I" is there both in the wonder and in the shame, both in "I am" and in "I will die." To let shame be pervaded by wonder is to unify the sense of "I." As I approach unity of being, I approach unity also of knowing and of loving, the unity, that is, of the known and the knower, of the loved and the lover. I am on "the road of the union of love with God." Unifying the sense of "I" answers the loneliness and the self-consciousness of our times. It answers the terror that arises from the isolation of the individual. Yet it is a process that remains incomplete, a road to be traveled still, because my sense of being known and loved is simply a sense of my heart being fathomed, not a fathoming of it myself, because the knowing and loving that comes of being known and loved is simply a knowing of One who knows, a loving of One who loves, not a fathoming of the heart that fathoms mine.

I believe I do have a glimpse of the secret nonetheless in this thought of shame pervaded by wonder. It is my clue to understanding the passion of Al-Hallaj and even to understanding the passion of Jesus. If I am on the right track here, the secret is in the unity of the subject, the sense of "I," and the unity comes about as the shame of "I will die" is pervaded by the wonder of "I am." Thus the passion of Jesus is at once personal and universal like his sense of "I," and we come to understand it by participating in it ourselves. The secret remains secret, even though I already know it, because I am still learning it, still learning to let shame be pervaded by wonder in my own life. I can feel heart's ease spreading in my life as I go on, and I know heart's ease is to be found in this unity, this sense of "I," for union within oneself is union also with God, and union with God is union also within oneself. It is being one with the One.

INDWELLING SOUL: A WAY TO LIVING IN GOD

There is a strange affinity between the mystic desire to unravel creation in returning to God and the apocalyptic desire to unleash nuclear energy. It is as if destruction, "brighter than a thousand suns," were a reversal of creation, at least in its story, going back from the created world to the founding act, "Let there be light." Mystic desire to go back to God takes the form of an unraveling of the sense of "I," as in Al-Hallaj's prayer,

"Betwixt me and Thee there lingers an 'it is I' that torments me. Ah, of Thy grace, take this 'I' from between us."[48] If union with God is relational, it is true, a unity of knowing and loving, and if selfhood is relational, "I know who am known" and "I love who am loved," then the return to God cannot really be destructive of self. What is really at issue is the separation from reality that is implied in knowing and loving, in taking reality into oneself in knowing and going out of oneself to reality in loving. If the separation were abolished, then reality would be in me, as in knowledge, and I would be in reality, as in love. There is a place in the heart where beloved images are kept, the place "in my heart where my soul dwells." To resolve my sense of "I" would be to go from images to reality.

A beloved image, as I am envisioning it, is the image I have in my heart of someone or something I love, as in Donne's Elegy,

> Here take my Picture; though I bid farewell,
> Thine, in my heart, where my soule dwels, shall dwell.

Or in his Holy Sonnet,

> Marke in my heart, O Soule, where thou dost dwell,
> The picture of Christ crucified, and tell . . .[49]

I think of the images I have seen in the places I have been, in Ayasofya where my eyes were drawn, each time I came in, to the image of the Madonna and Child in the apse, in the Rothko Chapel where I saw stations of the cross, as I believed, and yet images not of Christ himself but of what he was seeing and feeling in his passion, and here in the Meditation Room where "none of the symbols to which we are accustomed in our meditation could be used" since "people of many faiths will meet here," where "It is for those who come here to fill the void with what they find in their center of stillness."[50] I have gone from images of persons to images of what a person sees and feels to images of the void. Have I gone therefore from images to reality? And has all this been happening in my heart in the place where my soul dwells?

It occurs to me that the void itself is an image and not, as I would have thought, simply naked reality. "Void" or "emptiness" (*sunyata*) is the principal term in the Heart Sutra, a Buddhist scripture that begins with the words "Homage to the Perfection of Wisdom, the Lovely, the Holy!"[51] The void is the emptiness we can feel when we are alone and, once we have come upon it, can feel anywhere, even when we are among others. When we say "void" or "emptiness," we are giving expression to the feeling, forming an image of it. That is especially clear when the void becomes a beloved image, an image of heart's desire, as in the spell (*mantra*) of the Heart Sutra, "Gone, gone, gone beyond, gone altogether beyond, O what an awakening, all-hail!" Here again the mystic desire to unravel the sense of "I" and the apocalyptic desire to unravel the world are closely akin. Going back to the void in the story of creation means going back beyond even the founding act, "Let there be light," going altogether beyond to "The earth was without form and void, and darkness was on the face of the deep."[52] Still, there is wisdom there in the void, "the heart of Perfect Wisdom" according to Buddhist scriptures, the breath of God stirring the waters according to Hebrew scriptures, the figure of Wisdom playing before God.

No doubt, we usually flee from the void, seek to fill it with images, not beloved images, to be sure, but images that will distract us and make us forget the emptiness. I come to an end of a day's activity, but before I have a chance to encounter the void, to feel my own emptiness, I go to find entertainment. If I face the void, on the other hand, if I actually seek it, I am doing a dangerous and ambiguous thing. Let me see, as I sit here in the relative emptiness of the Meditation Room, coming back to my heart's longing, to the place "in my heart where my soul dwells," if I can discern between the mystic unraveling of the sense of "I" and the apocalyptic unraveling of the world, between thinking back to the void, remembering as it were, and actually trying to achieve the void.

I think of a dream a friend told me of recently, very similar to a dream Hammarskjold tells of in his diary:

> In a dream I walked with God through the deep places of creation; past walls that receded and gates that opened, through hall after hall of silence, darkness and refreshment—the dwelling place of souls ac-

quainted with light and warmth—until, around me, was an infinity into which we all flowed together and lived anew, like the rings made by raindrops falling upon wide expanses of calm dark waters.[53]

Here in a dream is the mystic unravling of the sense of "I," taking it from between person and person, from between person and God, resolving the "I" into "an infinity into which we all flowed together and lived anew." There is a going back through the story of creation, walking "with God through the deep places of creation," going back to the "light and warmth" of the first day and beyond to "calm dark waters." There is a going back to "the dwelling place of souls" like the place "in my heart where my soul dwells." There is no shame here, only wonder. It seems as if the sense of "I" has passed from an *opaque* phase of shame through a *translucent* phase of shame pervaded by wonder to a *transparent* phase where shame has been consumed in pure wonder.

I mention my friend's dream, without describing it, saying only that it was similar, simply because it helped me realize Hammarskjold's is a true dream. I can find in my own heart too the outlines of the longing that is being fulfilled here in the dream journey with God. Although I find myself trying to pass from the opaque to the translucent phase of "I" and not ready yet for the transparent phase, I do find hints of transparency in my life—these are my encounters with the figure of Wisdom. I suppose these hints occur because wonder is already an experience for me, because I do have a sense of being "grounded transparently,"[54] as Kierkegaard says, in God. Wonder for me is actually the earlier experience, deriving from childhood, preceding the shame I felt in the passing of youth. I guess that is why going forward to pure wonder, to transparent grounding, as in this dream, can seem to me like going back to the beginning.

It can also seem like going forward to the end, becoming grounded ever more transparently in God and ending at last in the vision of God in death. I think of the words describing the vision of God in the Bhagavad-Gita, "If the radiance of a thousand suns were to burst into the sky, that would be the splendor of the Mighty One."[55] It seems significant that these words are the epigraph to the story of nuclear discovery, *Brighter than a*

Thousand Suns. They suggest again the affinity of the mystic desire to dissolve the opacity of the self and let God shine through and the apocalyptic desire to dissolve the opacity of matter and to reveal the brightness of spirit. There is a deep connection between the two, I begin to see now, especially if matter is the "principle of individuation,"[56] as Aquinas says, the root of individuality. There is one and the same longing here, I think, expressing itself in terms of self and in terms of matter, seeking always the brightness of God, the brightness of spirit, but in danger always of looking for its fulfillment in the death of self, in the destruction of matter, rather than in the transparency of all individuality to the One.

If I consider the beloved images I have in my heart, it is true, I find it is not so easy to separate transparency from death and destruction. The very thought of a "vision of God in death" has them inseparably intertwined with each other. Of course, as I think on it, that may be the whole point of the middle phase of "I," the translucent phase, to let my mortality itself be permeated by light and to be on my way to transparency in death. That may be the point also of the words describing the vision of God in the New Testament, "For now we see through a glass, darkly; but then face to face: now I know in part; but then shall I know even as also I am known."[57] Here is a thread I can follow. Self and matter are opaque to begin with, and so are death and destruction, but they become translucent for me as I come to a sense of being known and loved, and they become transparent as I come to "know even as also I am known," to love even as also I am loved.

"We carry with us the wonders we seek without us,"[58] Browne says in *Religio Medici.* It is remarkable that he says this who also says "I am not so much afraid of death, as ashamed thereof." He is right, I carry with me the wonders I seek in Ayasofya, in the Rothko Chapel, and now in the Meditation Room. I carry them with me as beloved images "in my heart where my soul dwells." But do I carry them also as reality? That is the question that arises when I think of death. I carry with me the image of Mother and Child, of encompassing goodness and mercy, the image of what Christ sees and feels in human suffering and death, of joy that is deeper than sorrow, the image of the void whose "calm dark waters" are stirred by the breath of God, of quiet and simplicity that become union and ecstasy. But do I carry with me the reality of that goodness and mercy, of that joy, of that quiet and simplicity? I want to say "I do." To say that, however, is like saying "I do" in a wedding. It is saying "Yes" to God. It is a matter not of fact but of will, like making a last will and testament, of willingness, of saying "Yes" to goodness and mercy, "Yes" to joy, "Yes" to quiet and simplicity.

I do, therefore, and now I feel I am indeed passing from images to reality. I have come from memory to understanding to will. I do therefore I am. When Al-Hallaj is passing in this way, through understanding and willing, from the feeling of "illusion . . . illusion" to the feeling of "truth . . . truth," he comes to be convinced he will rise again in glory. Why? Massignon tells his story in questions, ending with this one, "Finally, why, during his last vigil in prison, did he doubt for such a long time, before understanding and crying out, that the fire in which his remains were going to be burned foretold the future glory of his resurrection?"[59] "God knows," Massignon answers, finding here the secret of the heart that remains secret. I begin to understand, nevertheless, as I pass from my memory of my life to my understanding of my own story in questions to my will, my "Yes," my "I do" resolving my own ambiguities.

All the paradoxes of life center, it seems, around one's relation to individuality, those of facing matter, those of facing self, those of facing death. I think of my own feeling about an otherworld, about solitude, about life as a journey in time. In relating to matter I am relating to the bodily roots of my own individuality; in relating to self I am relating to my individuality itself; and in relating to life ending in death I am relating to the process of my individuation, of living my individuality out in time. All of these things are inescapable, matter, self, life ending in death, but I am able to say "Yes" or "No" to them. My freedom is in my relating to them, my "Yes," my "I do." Although my feeling for the wonder of existence does lead me to say "Yes," my feeling for the shame of mortality leads me rather to say "No." If I do say "Yes" then, as I am doing, in spite of the shame, I am entering into the stance of Jesus "the pioneer and perfecter of our faith, who for the joy that was set before him endured the cross, despising the shame, and is seated at the right hand of the throne of God."[60] If I say "Yes," that is, I am willing, for the joy set before me, to endure death, in spite of the shame, in the hope of glory and resurrection. There is indeed a hint of joy beyond sorrow, of glory beyond shame, of resurrection beyond death in "Yes."

There is also a hint of transparency, only a hint, to be sure, for there is still an "in spite of." It is the transparency that comes of relating to self. By relating to myself and willing to be myself, as Kierkegaard says, I am "grounded transparently" in God. There is a further degree of transparency, though, that I have still to attain, that comes of relating to matter, to the root of my individuality, to my sexuality and my mortality, like Al-Hallaj unafraid of the loss of self that occurs in love and in death, willing to let go of the self I am still clutching to myself in shame. "The ecstatic wants only to be alone with his Only One,"[61] he cried out from the gibbet. That is full transparency, I believe, to want only to be one with the One in love and in death.

"I want to be eternally young in Him," he says of God, "eternally filled with desire, for He is the Essential Desire."[62] Heart's ease and heart's longing, he seems to be saying, are ultimately one and the same. I feel their difference rather, that between ease and unease, the ease of heart's ease and the unease of heart's longing. If they are ultimately one and the same, it has to be so "in my heart where my soul dwells." And so it is, I begin to believe, as I think of the beloved images I am keeping there, images of heart's desire, of what my heart desires, I mean, but reality of heart's desire itself, reality of actual desiring. As I go from images to reality, therefore, I go from the projections of my heart's longing back to the very longing itself. If I can find heart's ease in my heart's longing, if I can find "rest in restlessness,"[63] that is, then I too can say heart's ease and heart's longing are ultimately one and the same, I can even say God is "the Essential Desire." It is like saying God is my heart's desire. What I mean, nevertheless, is that God, instead of being an imaginative projection of my heart's longing, is the source of all such projection, that God dwells "in my heart where my soul dwells."

I find God when I go from images to reality, when I go back from imaginative projections to my heart's longing, not in every shape and form of longing, it is true, not in the "No" that turns it into a longing for death and destruction, but in the "Yes" that enables me to find heart's ease. So I may interpret the encompassing peace I found in Ayasofya, the peace in suffering and death I found in Rothko, the quiet and simplicity I find here in the Meditation Room. It is heart's ease in every instance, and it is heart's ease, I am thinking now, that comes of being at one with my heart's own longing. It is not that God is reducible to my heart's longing but rather that God's presence is felt in heart's ease. If I ask myself, therefore, the question I have been asking here in the Meditation Room, "What do I find in my center of stillness?", my answer has to be *heart's ease in heart's longing*.

Actually I find ease and unease in my heart's longing, rest and unrest. I imagine the unease, the unrest goes with the "in spite of" that is still there, with my "Yes" being mixed to some degree with "No." As I feel it, the unease is the divergence in my longing toward the Many, my wandering eye, wandering from person to person, my divided heart, divided between the way I have chosen to take and the ways I have not taken. If I look to the beloved images I carry "in my heart where my soul dwells," however, I gather there is a process by which images pass from the eyes to the heart. I think of my own image in the eye of another person,

> I fixe mine eye on thine, and there
> Pitty my picture burning in thine eye,
> My picture drown'd in a transparent teare,
> When I looke lower I espie; . . .

and then I think of my image passing into the other's heart,

> My picture vanish'd, vanish feares,
> . . . Though thou retaine of mee
> One picture more, yet that will bee,
> Being in thine owne heart, from all malice free.[64]

Something similar must happen as images pass from my own eyes to my own heart. There is a divergence, an ambivalence of envy and jealousy, while the image is there in my wandering eye, for my heart at this point is still divided, but there comes a convergence, a unity, when the image passes into my heart and becomes a beloved image.

Here then is my way, almost too simple a way, the passing of images from my eyes to my heart, the passing of images into my heart into the place where my soul dwells. It goes from seeing to feeling and on to the central core of feeling. It ends in my heart where God dwells. It is the way I have been following all along, I realize now, in Ayasofya, in the Rothko Chapel, and now in the Meditation Room. Does it imply God and the soul are one and the same? I am thinking of the two phrases I have been using, "in my heart where my soul dwells" and "in my heart where God dwells." No, as I bring seeing and feeling together in my soul, I find rather a union of God and soul, I find God is here rather as in Max Jacob's witty exclamations, "My eye is God!" and "My heart is God's barrel!", as if God were seeing with my eyes and feeling with my heart or I were seeing with God's eyes and feeling with God's heart.

To be "in my heart where my soul dwells," nevertheless, is to be where I keep beloved images. It is to be where I feel my heart's desire. There, when I am dwelling there myself, my sense of "I" is true. It is there, no doubt, dwelling there, that Al-Hallaj was inspired to say "I am the truth." I think again of the words "God is love, and he who abides in love abides in God, and God abides in him."[65] Abiding in love is dwelling "where my soul dwells," "where God dwells." There the separation seems to be abolished between self and reality in knowing and loving. When I am dwelling in my mind, the separation still exists in knowing, for I am taking reality into myself. When I am dwelling in my heart but not yet in my soul, the separation still exists in loving, for I am going out of myself to reality. As images pass from my eyes into my heart into my soul, though, I myself go from dwelling in my mind to dwelling in my heart to dwelling in my soul. There in my soul I am no longer taking reality into myself but reality dwells in me; I am no longer going out of myself to reality but I dwell in reality. Self dwelling in soul is self dwelling in God. Knowing is God abiding in me. Loving is my abiding in God.

Knowing, it has been said, is always an indwelling, a dwelling in the particulars of what is known. "Understanding," Michael Polanyi says, "is based on our dwelling in the particulars of that which we comprehend."[66] That is true, it seems, of knowing that comes of loving, for loving is a going out to reality and ultimately a dwelling in reality. In knowing then my dwelling in reality becomes reality dwelling in me. Thus my dwelling in the particulars of Ayasofya, of the Rothko Chapel, of the Meditation Room, becomes the indwelling of those particulars in me, the indwelling of beloved images, the indwelling of soul. That does not seem true, however, of knowing without loving. "Things which we can tell," Polanyi says, "we know by observing them; those that we cannot tell, we know by dwelling in them." Actually I have begun in each instance by observing and ended by dwelling in the particulars of what I have been telling, as images pass from my eyes into my heart and soul.

Loving, therefore, is what makes it possible to pass from observing them to dwelling in them. When I am on the other end of observing, when I am being observed myself, I have the feeling of shame, of being known but not loved. When I am on the other end of indwelling, however, when the presence is in me, I have the sense of being known and loved, of my heart being fathomed. As it is, my own observing has been aimed at indwelling and my indwelling has been in the reality I have found of being known and loved, of encompassing peace, of joy underlying sorrow, of quiet and simplicity. So my knowing has become loving and my loving has become knowing. "Now contemplation and desire, united into one, inhabit a world where every beloved image has bodily form, and every bodily form is loved,"[67] as Yeats says in *A Vision*, describing what he calls "unity of being." Every beloved image has bodily form for me in Ayasofya, in the Rothko Chapel, and here in the Meditation Room, and every bodily form is loved, but for me every beloved image points beyond itself, as time is "a changing image of eternity," and every bodily form suggests resurrection in glory.

Unity of being, as I understand it, is unity of the sense of "I," and it comes of "Yes" rather than "No." There is a mystic "Yes," inspired by the wonder of existence, that would render all individuality transparent to God, I have found, and there is an apocalyptic "No," inspired by the shame of mortality, that would destroy matter, the root of individuality. Still, if true apocalypse is revelation, it is realized in transparency rather than in destruction. "No" is at work in me and in the world at large and will come to its end along with "Yes." All the same I can hope "No" is swallowed up in "Yes," shame is swallowed up in wonder, "death is swallowed up in victory."[68]

NOTES

1. Gertrude Stein, *Reflection on the Atomic Bomb*, ed. Robert Bartlett Hass (Los Angeles: Black Sparrow, 1973), p. 161.
2. Eckhart's word is *gelazenheit*, in modern German *Gelassenheit*. Cf. Reiner Schürmann, *Meister Eckhart: Mystic and Philosopher* (Bloomington, Ind.: Indiana University Press, 1978), pp. 16–17, 111, 185–186, and especially 191–213 (comparison with Heidegger). Cf. Martin Heidegger, *Discourse on Thinking* (German title: *Gelassenheit*), trans. John M. Anderson and E. Hans Freund (New York: Harper & Row, 1969), p. 54 (cf. pp. 61–62 where Eckhart is mentioned).
3. Heidegger, *Discourse on Thinking*, p. 53.
4. Dag Hammarskjold, "A Room of Quiet" (New York: The United Nations, 1971), the last sentence.
5. Shakespeare, *Hamlet*, Act I, scene 1, line 112 and scene 2, lines 184–185.
6. Ibid., Act III, scene 1, line 56.
7. Cf. the prologue to Heidegger's *Being and Time*, trans. John Macquarrie and Edward Robinson (New York: Harper, 1962), p. 1, and his dissertation on Duns Scotus, *Die kategorien und bedeutungslehre des Duns Scotus* (Tübingen: Mohr, 1916).
8. Ludwig Wittgenstein, *Tractatus Logico-Philosophicus*, 6.44, ed. D. F. Pears and B. F. McGuinness (London: Routledge & Kegan Paul, 1961), p. 148 (my translation). Cf. my use of this sentence in *The Church of the Poor Devil* (New York: Macmillan, 1982), p. 128.
9. Herman Kahn, *Thinking about the Unthinkable* (New York: Horizon, 1962).
10. Vladimir Solovyov, "Three Meetings," trans. Ralph Koprince in Carl and Ellendea Proffer (eds.), *The Silver Age of Russian Culture* (Ann Arbor, Mich.: Ardis, 1975), p. 132, and Robert Jungk, *Brighter than a Thousand Suns*, trans. James Cleugh (New York: Harcourt Brace, 1958).
11. Herman Melville, *Moby Dick* (New York: New American Library, 1961), p. 535.
12. Wittgenstein, *Tractatus*, 6.45 (p. 148) (my translation).
13. Solovyov, "Three Meetings," p. 132.
14. Luke 11:49.
15. It is the second antiphon at Morning Prayer on Saturday in the Third Week of Ordinary Time in *The Liturgy of the Hours* (New York: Catholic Book Publishing Co., 1975), 3:1109 and 4:1073.

16. J. R. R. Tolkien, *The Lord of the Rings* (London: Allen & Unwin, 1969), pp. 702–703. The phrase "Standing Silence" is used on p. 991.
17. John Donne, "Goe and catche a falling starre" in *The Poems of John Donne*, ed. Herbert Grierson (London: Oxford University Press, 1960), p. 8.
18. Saint Augustine, *Confessions* (Book X, Chapter 16), trans. R. S. Pine-Coffin (New York: Penguin, 1961), p. 223.
19. Luke 20:38.
20. Soren Kierkegaard, *The Point of View of My Work as an Author*, trans. Walter Lowrie (New York: Oxford University Press, 1939), p. 66n.
21. Luke 2:14.
22. Bo Beskow, *Dag Hammarskjold: Strictly Personal* (Garden City, N.Y.: Doubleday, 1969), p. 181.
23. Vladimir Solovyov, *Three Conversations*, trans. Alexander Bakshy under the title *War, Progress, and the End of History* (London: University of London, 1915), p. xix.
24. Joel 2:28 and Acts 2:17.
25. Vladimir Solovyov, *Plato*, trans. Richard Gill (with note on Solovyov by Janko Lavrin) (London: Stanley Nott, 1935), especially the discussion of tragedy, pp. 43ff., and the conclusion, pp. 80–83.
26. Matthew 6:22–23. Cf. Luke 11:34–36.
27. Matthew 20:15 (RSV note = King James). Cf. Mark 7:22 (King James).
28. Cf. my discussion of Joseph Conrad's *Heart of Darkness* (New York: Penguin, 1978), in *The Church of the Poor Devil*, pp. 4–17, and cf. Robert Jay Lifton on "spiritual numbness" in his book on the survivors of Hiroshima, *Death in Life* (New York: Random House, 1967), pp. 500–510.
29. On the meaning of Al-Hallaj's name, see Herbert Mason's preface to his play *The Death of Al-Hallaj* (Notre Dame, Ind.: University of Notre Dame Press, 1979), p. vii. For Massignon's saying, see Mason's forward to his translation of Louis Massignon, *The Passion of Al-Hallaj* (Princeton, N.J.: Princeton University Press, 1982), 1: xix, and also Massignon's own preface, 1: 1xv.
30. Compare the passage on mind's eye in *The Cloud of Unknowing*, trans. Clifton Wolters (Harmondsworth, England: Penguin, 1961), p. 58 with that in Eckhart, *Defensio*, IX, 19, trans. Raymond B. Blakney, in *Meister Eckhart* (New York: Harper & Row, 1941), p. 288.
31. Matthew 6:23.
32. Massignon quotes Al-Hallaj's saying "I am the truth" in the 1914 Foreword (p. 1i) and writes the dedication in Latin (my translation here) above the 1921 Foreword (p. 1) of *The Passion of Al-Hallaj*, vol. 1. The saying of Jesus is in John 14:6.
33. Shakespeare, *Romeo and Juliet*, Act IV, scene 5, lines 102–107. Cf. *Henry V*, Act IV, scene 1, lines 256–257 and *Julius Caesar*, Act I, scene 2, lines 207–208.
34. Dag Hammarskjold, *Markings*, trans. Leif Sjöberg and W. H. Auden (New York: Knopf, 1964), p. 216.
35. Franz Kafka, *Tagebücher* (New York: Schocken, 1949), p. 475 (my translation). Cf. my discussion of this passage in *The Reasons of the Heart* (New York: Macmillan, 1978), pp. 5–6.
36. Luke 11:49.
37. Sir Thomas Browne, *Religio Medici*, ed. Jean-Jacques Denonain (Cambridge: At the University Press, 1955), p. 53.
38. Genesis 3:5.

39. Mason, *The Death of Al-Hallaj*, p. 18.
40. Massignon, *The Passion of Al-Hallaj*, vol. 1, p. 13.
41. Cf. my discussion of the Shekinah and the "I am" sayings in *The Reasons of the Heart*, pp. 50–51 and the reference to the conversation with David Daube in 1970 in footnote 19 on p. 157. I spoke with him about it again in 1984. Cf. Daube's discussion of the "I am" in his book *The New Testament and Rabbinic Judaism* (London: University of London, Athlone Press, 1956), pp. 325–329.
42. A condemned proposition of Eckhart's in the papal bull "In agro dominico" (March 27, 1329) in *Meister Eckhart*, trans. Edmund Colledge and Bernard McGinn (New York: Paulist Press, 1981), p. 78.
43. The conversation was in the summer of 1980 on Cape Cod at a talk he gave in the Wellfleet Conference of that year. Cf. Erik Erickson, "The Galilean Sayings and the Sense of 'I'" in *Yale Review* (Spring 1981), pp. 321–362, and especially p. 358 ("individuality and universality"). (In our conversation, where I mentioned David Daube's view that the "I am" is an expression of the Shekinah, he said "both transcendent and personal.")
44. Cf. Massignon, *The Passion of Al-Hallaj*, vol. 3, pp. 219–221.
45. T. S. Eliot, "Burnt Norton," lines 42–43 in *Four Quartets* (New York: Harcourt, Brace & World, 1971), p. 14.
46. Max Jacob, "Cosmogonie" in *Le cornet a des* (Paris: Gallimard, 1945), p. 194 (my translation). Cf. also the translation in Max Jacob, *The Dice Cup*, ed. Michael Brownstein (New York: SUN, 1979), p. 75 and the translation and discussion in Gerald Kamber, *Max Jacob and the Poetics of Cubism* (Baltimore: Johns Hopkins, 1971), pp. 5–7.
47. Rainer Maria Rilke, *The Notebooks of Malte Laurids Brigge*, trans. M. D. Herter Norton (New York: Norton, 1964), p. 216.
48. Al-Hallaj's prayer is translated by R. A. Nicholson in Mircea Eliade, *From Primitives to Zen* (New York: Harper & Row, 1967), p. 524.
49. Donne, Elegy V in *The Poems of John Donne*, p. 77, and Holy Sonnet XIII, ibid., p. 299.
50. Hammarskjold, "A Room of Quiet."
51. Edward Conze, *Buddhist Wisdom Books* (London: Allen & Unwin, 1966), p. 77 (also the beginning of the Diamond Sutra, p. 21) and pp. 101–102 (*mantra*) and p. 102 ("the heart of Perfect Wisdom").
52. Genesis 1:3 and 1:2.
53. Hammarskjold, *Markings*, p. 118.
54. Cf. Kierkegaard's formula quoted earlier in this book in Chapter 5, note 15.
55. Bhagavad-Gita 11:12 as epigraph of Robert Jungk's book on the personal history of the atomic scientists, *Brighter than a Thousand Suns*, p. vii.
56. Saint Thomas Aquinas, *De Ente et Essentia* (Chapter 2), ed. C. Boyer (Rome: Gregoriana, 1946), p. 17 (*individuationis principium est materia*).
57. I Corinthians 13:12 (King James).
58. Browne, *Religio Medici*, p. 21.
59. Massignon, *The Passion of Al-Hallaj*, vol. 1, p. lxvi.
60. Hebrews 12:2.
61. Mason, *The Death of Al-Hallaj*, p. 80.
62. Ibid., p. 21.
63. "Rest in restlessness" is my formula in *Time and Myth* (Garden City, N.Y.: Doubleday, 1973), p. 79.

64. Donne, "Witchcraft by a Picture," in *The Poems of John Donne*, p. 41.
65. I John 4:16.
66. Michael Polanyi, *Personal Knowledge* (New York: Harper & Row, 1964), p. x (in the preface to the Torchbook edition).
67. W. B. Yeats, *A Vision* (New York: Collier-Macmillan, 1966), p. 136.
68. I Corinthians 15:54, referring to Isaiah 25:8.

7. A Symbol Resolved

on walking in the
woods at World's End

What if the world ends in beauty and in golden light? That is the thought that comes to me by surprise as I walk here in the late afternoon with a friend. We came, attracted by the romance of the name, World's End.[1] Actually it is a peninsula and a forest reservation near Hingham in Massachusetts. As I walk in these woods, I think of the beginning of the human story, of God "walking in the garden in the cool of the day,"[2] and I think maybe the end will be like the beginning, after shame ("and the man and his wife hid themselves from the presence of the Lord") is consumed in wonder.

In the beginning, according to the story of Adam and Eve, human beings walked and spoke with God; in the end, I think as I walk here with my friend, we will walk again with God in beauty and in golden light. Here I come once more upon the symbol of my life, a journey with God in time, "an unresolved symbol" I called it, only now I imagine us walking with God in a timeless peace. I seem to have resolved the symbol of a journey in time into that of walking in light and in beauty. I expected to resolve the symbol into the reality, and so I have in a way, by making an actual journey in time, going from place to place, a pilgrimage, a reality indeed and one that has led me into a new reality, the encompassing peace I have found, the joy underlying sorrow, the quiet and the simplicity. A sympathetic reader of mine has challenged me on the symbolism of the journey, on that of solitude, too, and on that of an otherworld, on how true such symbolism is to life. All those symbols are resolved here, it seems to me, at journey's end, at solitude's end, and indeed at world's end.

What is it to resolve a symbol? It is to pass from symbol to reality, no doubt, but it is to do so, I believe, by gaining insight into image. An insight does not take away the image. It is rather a realizing that the image is an image, a rendering of the symbol translucent or even transparent. An insight into a journey with God in time, for instance, does not take away the journey. It is rather a realizing that the journey is with God and not simply toward God, that solitude is being alone with the Alone and not simply being alone, that an otherworld is a deeper life we live already now and not simply a life after life. So if I say my journey with God in time resolves into walking with God in light and in beauty, I am speaking in images like those in the Navaho chant,

> I walk with beauty before me,
> with beauty behind me, with beauty above me,
> with beauty below me, with beauty all around me.[3]

That has been my experience of God on this pilgrimage, before me, behind me, above me, below me, all around me, God as beauty, God as light. My experience of "inward peace," as Al-Alawi calls it, has been one of encompassing goodness and mercy; my experience of "self-realization in God" has been one of living in God.

I am speaking in images, like that of standing in the hollow of a giant redwood tree, as I have actually done, but am living in the insight, in the awareness of image as image. Speaking in images, I think of "The Deer's Cry," the ancient Celtic invocation of Christ as a shield against danger,

> Christ with me, Christ before me, Christ behind me,
> Christ in me, Christ beneath me, Christ above me,
> Christ on my right, Christ on my left . . .[4]

Living in insight, in the awareness of image as image, I think of being in God, of love, and of God being in me, of knowledge, and of the knowing that comes of loving,

> Wisdom of God,
> Be with me,
> Always at work in me.

My song is of knowledge and love, therefore, of knowing that comes of loving. That is the truth in my poetry, the reality in my symbolism. *Wisdom is knowing that comes of loving.* It is a conjoining of knowledge and love that I have been trying to find, first of all, in human embodiments, as "a person in the persons" I have known. I encounter it whenever "heart speaks to heart," whenever a person who loves me seems also for a moment to know me, to fathom my heart. That seems especially to happen when I am trying to fathom the heart of the other, to "pass over," as I call it, into the other's life. Instead of fathoming, I am fathomed. Instead of knowing and loving, I am known and loved. Maybe being known and being loved is the beginning of knowing and loving, and maybe you have to pass over into the other's knowing and loving to feel known and loved yourself. Anyway it is in those moments of heart speaking to heart that I feel known and loved by God, even though it is human heart speaking to human heart. For God alone, it seems to me as I try in vain to fathom it myself, can penetrate the heart's secret. It is God who knows in our knowing, who loves in our loving.

Seeing with God's eyes and feeling with God's heart, or God seeing with our eyes and feeling with our heart, this has been my metaphor of union of God and soul. It is an image of knowing with God's knowing and loving with God's loving, or of God knowing in our knowing and loving in our loving. Here is the figure of Wisdom. It is what I understand by "a person in the persons." Wisdom is God's eyes and heart, as when God says of the Temple, "my eyes and my heart will be there for all time,"[5] and she comes to be in human eyes and a human heart, to dwell in a human body as a temple, and a human being can say, as from the burning bush, "I am." Here is the figure of Christ. It is what I understand by "the Word became flesh and dwelt among us" and "we have beheld his glory."[6] According to the makers of icons, only angels and prophets were allowed to see the glory of God before the coming of Christ, but now we are all able to see.[7]

As I understand it, if we conjoin seeing and feeling, there is a reality we may come to experience, "That which was from the beginning, which we have heard, which we have seen with our eyes, which we have looked upon and touched with our hands, concerning the Word of life."[8] I have been going from place to

place on my pilgrimage, from Ayasofya to the Rothko Chapel
to the Meditation Room at the United Nations, looking for that
reality. As it turns out, I have come to it more in my awareness
than in my perception, more in my seeing and my feeling than
in what I have seen and felt. Seeing and feeling are sense, it is
true; knowing and loving are spirit; and yet seeing is pervaded
by knowing and feeling is pervaded by loving. Sense is pervaded
by spirit, and that is how I have come to understand what "we
have heard," what "we have seen with our eyes," what "we have
looked upon and touched with our hands." Christ to me has
been the subject rather than the object. I enter into his relationship with God, I mean, seeing with his eyes and feeling with
his heart. Thus he is "with me, before me, behind me, in me,
beneath me, above me, on my right, on my left."

My starting point has been knowing that takes reality in and
loving that goes out to reality; my ending point has been reality
dwelling in me by knowing and my dwelling in reality by loving.
I have gone from God as "It is," as in Eckhart's "Existence is
God" and Gandhi's "Truth is God," to God as "I am," as in
Exodus and in John's Gospel, taking the sense of "I" in the
sayings of Jesus to be personal to him and yet universal to all,
something I can enter into, therefore, by seeing with his eyes,
feeling with his heart, entering thus into his unity with God,
seeing with God's eyes, feeling with God's heart. So if there is
"an understanding in the discoveries" I have made, it has become ever more personal, ever more universal, ever more "personal knowledge," ever more "insight." God has become eyes
and heart to me.

Starting from a knowing and a loving still separated from
reality, I started with the thought of a journey, of solitude, of
an otherworld, images of my own standing over and against
reality. Aiming at union with reality, though, union really of
God and soul, at journey's end, at solitude's end, at world's end,
I have gone from place to place on my pilgrimage, looking for
a knowing that will be God's eyes and a loving that will be God's
heart, looking always for a place where God can say, as of the
Temple, "my eyes and my heart will be there for all time." Yet
place seems always to vanish in significance, along with all the
particulars I see and feel there, before the seeing and the feel-

ing, before the knowing and the loving. I came first to Ayasofya in Istanbul, hoping to meet Holy Wisdom herself there, going a long and solitary journey into a world other than my own, much like Solovyov as I learned afterwards when I read his poem. And so I did meet her, not on the side of the object, to be sure, but on that of the subject, not as a figure appearing to me in a vision, I mean, as Solovyov saw her, but as new eyes and a new heart. Still, I did see the light in Ayasofya with those new eyes and feel the encompassing peace there with that new heart, and so I thought I was able to say to her, like Solovyov, "Before me, in me—were you alone."

"Before me," not as a figure appearing in a vision but simply as light shining in a dark place, seen by seeing conjoined with feeling, "in me," as inward peace but encompassing me all around, felt by feeling conjoined with seeing, "were you alone," as knowing in my seeing, as loving in my feeling, as knowing that is loving, as loving that is knowing. Again those preposi-tional phrases "before me, in me" suggest a relational unity, like "Christ with me, Christ before me, Christ behind me, Christ in me . . .," but the words "were you alone" suggest an accord, at least in that moment, my eyes according to God's eyes, my heart according to God's heart. All I can think of now is my eyes wandering, my heart divided. Still, I can invoke Holy Wisdom "before me, in me" as I can invoke Christ "with me, before me, behind me, in me . . ." Maybe that is the truth of my journey's end, my solitude's end, my world's end, a relational unity.

It all becomes clearer to me when I pass over, as I did at Ayasofya, into the Muslim faith in the absolute unity of God, "There is no god but God," when I enter into the seeing implied in the words of the Koran inscribed inside the dome of Ayaso-fya, "God is the Light of the heavens and the earth," when I enter into the feeling implied in the words of Rumi, "The lovers of God have no religion but God alone." It is very clear in Islam that we are on one side and God is on the other side of our relationship with God, that God is the Light and we have eyes to see the Light, that God is the beloved and we are the lovers who have the heart to love God. When I come back again to Christianity, I realize God is on both sides of our relationship with God, according to my faith in Jesus as the Son of God, that God is eyes to me as well as light, that God is heart to me as well as beloved. There is not only the absolute unity, "In the name of Allah, the compassionate, the merciful," but also the relational unity, "In the name of the Father and of the Son and of the Holy Spirit." We can enter into the relational unity, even though we always fall short of the absolute unity, always remain other than God.

We always fall short, always remain other, and yet are always on the way, I am always on the way, it seems, on this pilgrimage, to having eyes according to God's eyes, to having a heart according to God's heart. My wandering eyes, my divided heart make me realize the truth of Van Gogh's words, "I cannot dispense with something greater than myself." He can dispense with God on the side of the object, as a theme of painting, but he cannot dispense with God on the side of the subject, as "the power of creating." I see a pitfall here, nevertheless, for myself and for secular modernity, wanting to dispense with God as the Light, with God as the beloved, and to have God only as eyes and heart. Somehow I have to go beyond the vision of secular modernity, the vision that stops at the reality of human existence in time, and use God's eyes and heart to see the glory, like the makers of icons, to see "that something of the eternal," as Van Gogh calls it, to see time as "a changing image of eternity."

After I came back from Ayasofya, therefore, I began "a wanderyear of soul," as I called it, learning to use God's eyes and heart, learning to see meaning, that is, and to feel presence. What I had already learned at Ayasofya was to conjoin seeing and feeling. I experimented now with separating them from one another, or with the thought of separating them, just to see what it meant to conjoin them. I found there is a deep-going tendency to separate them in our times. There is a madness at work in our times, I have begun to realize, that comes of seeing without feeling, and there is a terror and a despair at work too that come of feeling without seeing:

> Cast a cold eye
> On life, on death.
> Horseman, pass by![9]

Those words of Yeats, meant for his own epitaph, are an epitaph of our times. They evoke both seeing and feeling, side by side, seeing without feeling, though, "a cold eye on life, on death," and feeling without seeing, "Horseman, pass by!"

As I look into "a cold eye," as I see my own image, my life and death, reflected there, I realize suddenly what seeing without feeling really is. It is knowing without loving. When I say "really," I am thinking again of sense pervaded by spirit. Seeing without feeling is knowing without loving, and we hide ourselves from it in shame. We hide ourselves from the presence of God, "and the man and his wife hid themselves from the presence of the Lord," when we have become aware of being naked to seeing without feeling, when the knowing we know is a knowing without loving. What is it then to conjoin seeing and feeling, I have asked myself, to conjoin knowing and loving? It is to open ourselves to the presence of God, I believe, no longer to hide ourselves but to be naked to "the presence of the Lord." And so, as being known and loved becomes knowing and loving, as being seen becomes seeing, it is to see with an eye like that of Brother Lawrence seeing the tree in winter, knowing it would put forth leaves, blossom, and bear fruit in spring. It is to see what "a cold eye on life, on death" cannot see, the presence of God in life, in death.

Presence of mind, and not of mind only but of heart and soul, that is what it means, I think, to conjoin seeing and feeling, God's presence to us then, our presence to one another, my presence to myself in conjoining them. Presence takes away not only the madness of our seeing without feeling but also the terror and the despair of our feeling without seeing. Those words, "Horseman, pass by!" make me think of the Four Horsemen of the Apocalypse, of war and famine and sickness and death, of eyes averted, of overwhelming feeling, of power that is in terror and despair. All I have to set against terror and despair is presence, and yet presence, I do believe, is enough, for "a timeless presence in time," God's to us, ours to one another, mine to myself, becomes "a meaning in unmeaning things of life." Our meeting with God, our meeting with one another, my meeting with myself, is always more, that is, than a chance meeting.

Indeed if "all real living is meeting," as Buber says, then the presence at work in life, the presence of God, of human beings, of self, is the real substance of life. It is what is really happening in my life and even in my times. Here too, when I say "really," I am thinking of sense pervaded by spirit, of presence found in knowing and in loving. If I say "Things are meant," therefore, as I have been saying, I am speaking not of the madness of our times, not of the terror and the despair, as if they too were meant, but of the presence at work in my life and in our lives, and so in my times and in our times, working against the madness, against the terror and the despair. I am thinking ultimately of the presence of Christ, the *parousia*, taking the word in its primary sense, "presence," even more than in its secondary sense, "coming," thinking of Christ "with me, before me, behind me, in me, beneath me, above me, on my right, on my left," of the words "I am with you always, even unto the end of the world,"[10] taking the world's end, as I am doing here, in terms of "I am with you."

There are signs of our times, I believe, signs of presence, just as in New Testament times there were signs of coming. The signs of presence, though, are like the stations of the cross in the Rothko Chapel, dark panels in black and red, where we do not see Christ but we see what he is seeing and feel what he is feeling. Thus it was I came to Rothko on my pilgrimage. At Ayasofya I was looking for God's eyes and heart, thinking of the words "my eyes and my heart will be there for all time." At Rothko I found myself looking for the human eyes and heart of Christ. When I had first visited the chapel some years before, I had thought I was seeing despair in those dark paintings, knowing Mark Rothko had committed suicide. It is what one would think simply observing the madness, the terror, and the despair of our times. Now on my pilgrimage I saw instead a deep-running insight into human suffering and death.

It is an insight, a seeing, I felt as peace and a peace, a feeling, I saw as insight. I thought of the words "the peace of God which passes all understanding."[11] It passes all understanding because understanding fails us when we come up against human suffering and death. Yet the peace I saw in those dark panels was luminous. There is an understanding that comes out of the peace itself, an understanding that passes all understanding! I saw it and felt it not when I was sitting on the benches of the chapel, gazing at the panels, it is true, but when I was walking from panel to panel as from station to station, making the stations of the cross, saying to myself at each one the traditional words "We adore thee O Christ and we bless thee, because by thy holy cross thou hast redeemed the world." I saw it and felt it, I mean, not by observing the paintings but by entering into the human suffering and death I thought they were showing, by entering, as far as I could, into the suffering and death of Christ. Thus it seemed to me I was seeing with his eyes and feeling with his heart.

Entering into human suffering and death, I realize now, is a dangerous undertaking, especially living day after day with suffering and death weighing on your mind. It can numb you, leaving you in the cold of seeing without feeling, and it can blind you, leaving you in the dark of feeling without seeing. I think of Mark Rothko himself and of his suicide. Still, the cold gives way to the warmth, the dark gives way to the light in the human eyes and heart of Christ. Seeing with those eyes, I can see in the dark of our feeling, and feeling with that heart, I can feel in the cold of our seeing. The light and the warmth are in the eyes and heart, I begin to realize, more than in the suffering and death that are seen and felt. It is the light of knowing that redeems us from the dark, and it is the warmth of loving that redeems us from the cold.

Seeing in the dark of our feeling means seeing hope and courage, or seeing lives of hope and courage, in dark times when, as in Thoreau's times, "The mass of men live lives of quiet desperation."[12] Feeling in the cold of our seeing means entering into what we see, even into human suffering and death, in times when "an extreme critical lucidity," as Polanyi calls it, is set over and against "an intense moral conscience"[13] on suffering and death. So if I say "There are signs," as I have been doing, I am speaking of entering into human suffering and death and finding hope and courage, of us entering and us finding, I mean, and of those who enter and those who find who are signs to us, and of having the heart to enter and the eyes to find, of having the heart and the eyes of Christ. I think of figures of our times and of times past, of Max Jacob, of Vladimir Solovyov, of Ramon Lull, of Al-Hallaj, all of them in love with God, as it seems, all of them entering somehow into the figure of Christ so that the figure itself disappears, as in the stations at Rothko, and all that is left is the dark red and black of human suffering and death suffused with the light and warmth of hope and courage. As light shining in our darkness and warmth glowing in our coldness, I believe, it is the light and warmth of a true passing through death to life.

As I come back to myself from the passing I found at Rothko, I wondered, nevertheless, how true it is to life and to death. I was waiting for my heart to speak. My eyes were leading me as I went from station to station, finding signs of life, of joy, of reality. Now my heart must lead me. There is something wild about those figures that are signs to me, I realized, that are in love with God, that meld with the figure of Christ, something wild about their words, about their vision of life. Max Jacob is wild; Vladimir Solovyov is wild; Ramon Lull is wild; Al-Hallaj is wild; and I become wild too if I join them. I thought of Ramon Lull calling himself "Fool of Love." That is it, love, I concluded, a love that is stronger than death, and my own heart responds to it, rises to it as to an inspiration. When I say "wild," I mean untame, undomesticated by life. Death too, I know, is untame, undomesticated, but love is stronger.

It is the love that comes of being loved that is stronger, the love that is "from God and of God and towards God" in the words of the old man whom Lawrence met in the desert of Arabia, another of those wild figures, I imagine, who are in love with God. When I reflect on that sentence, "The love is from God and of God and towards God," and on all the extravagant sayings of those who are in love with God, like the words of Ramon Lull on the human "lover" and the divine "beloved" and on himself as "Fool of Love," I can see there is indeed a deeper life that is going on in that loving and being loved, in that "from and of and towards," again those prepositional phrases that speak of relation, a life of relation that does seem capable of living on through death, of going on where everyday life must come to an end. It is as if the lover of God has a secret life—Lull is always talking about the "secrets" of the lover and the beloved. I finally looked at the original Catalan to find the word he is using, and I found it is exactly the same in English, except in pronunciation, *secrets*.[14] The word suggests to me an unknown life, a mysterious life, the very thing that draws one human being to another in love, seeing a mysterious life in another and hoping to share in it.

As for myself, I face a choice here, whether to give my heart to "the road of the union of love with God," the road I have been walking on this pilgrimage, or to keep thinking of other possible loves, of roads I have not taken. Here is where "The heart speaks," as I have been saying, speaks as always for the mysterious life you find in other persons, speaks with all its voice, though, for the love that is "with all your heart, and with all your soul, and with all your might." It seems there is a unity of language, as in a lover's discourse, in the heart's speaking, "a word in the words," and there is a unity of vision, as in the "light-bearing eyes" of an artist, in the eyes' seeing, "a view in the viewpoints." It is the relational unity I have been coming upon, the "from and of and towards," the "with me, before me, behind me, in me, beneath me, above me, on my right, on my left." It is a unity of loving and of knowing.

These are the two basic ways we have of relating to the things of life, knowing and loving, and they are related to one another, I have been finding, the knowing comes of the loving. By knowing we take things into ourselves; by loving we go out of ourselves to the persons and the situations in our life. Or so it is the beginning. In the end all we know dwells in us and we dwell in all we love. Knowing and loving God, though, still has to do with the things of life, for it means looking into God's eyes, as it were, and entering into God's heart, and so ultimately it means seeing the things of life with God's eyes and feeling them with God's heart. It never means turning away from the things of life. It is like looking into the eyes of another human being— what you see there is a reflected image of what the eyes are seeing. So it is too with entering into the heart of another— what you feel there is what the other is feeling. On "the road of the union of love with God," therefore, you do not turn away from the persons and the situations of your life, I gather, even though you make a choice for that road, as I am trying to do now, and turn away from other possible loves, from roads you are not taking. Instead you find somehow on the road of union a unity of seeing and of feeling.

Spirit in sense, knowing in seeing and loving in feeling, that is the way I have been following. Or then again, "That which was from the beginning, which we have heard, which we have seen with our eyes, which we have looked upon and touched with our hands, concerning the Word of life," the way that Christ is, that is the way I have been following. Thus I began at Ayasofya looking for God's eyes and heart, and I went on at Rothko to look for the human eyes and heart of Christ. I came in the end, however, in the Meditation Room at the United Nations to look for my own eyes and heart. For if we see with God's eyes and feel with God's heart in the union of God and soul, I realized, then God sees with our eyes and feels with our heart. It is not like the lovers in Nathaniel Hawthorne's story who "had looked love" and "spoken love"[15] to each other but did not dare touch one another, two persons facing each other but never becoming one in love.

It is more like lovers dwelling in one another, looking into but then seeing with each other's eyes, speaking to but then feeling with each other's hearts. Still, using my eyes and my heart, as I have been doing, I am always in danger of merely looking and speaking love. All I can hope is that looking and speaking will lead, as it does even in Hawthorne's story, to sharing, to the reality of a union that depends finally on my "Yes," my "I do." Here is the way I have been following, saying "There is a way," from looking love to speaking love to sharing life, from my eyes to my heart to the place "in my heart where my soul dwells," from knowing to loving to knowing that comes of loving. It is the way, I thought in the Meditation Room, not only of my life but also of my times. Starting with my eyes, with "mind's eye" really, with the knowing in our seeing, I did not at first find God knowing in our knowing. I thought I found rather the ambiguity of our vision, oscillating, as in an optical illusion, between a mystic vision of our creation and an apocalyptic vision of our destruction. It seemed to me to reflect the ambiguity of the human heart, oscillating between the wonder of existence and the dread and fascination of death.

As I entered then into the ambiguity of the human heart, the darkness actually of my own heart, I thought I found shame at the heart of our dread and our fascination, saying with Sir Thomas Browne "I am not so much afraid of death, as ashamed thereof," and so I thought "heart's ease" comes of a consuming of shame in wonder. Here I believe I do find God loving in our loving. For whenever human love penetrates our shame, it seems always more than human love, wiser than human love. For if shame comes of knowing without loving, the love that penetrates shame is a loving that is knowing and its wisdom is a knowing that is loving. As I sat, therefore, in "a room of quiet where only thoughts should speak," I realized thoughts could be those of knowing without loving, the thoughts that speak to our shame, that leave us opaque, and they could be those of knowing that is loving and loving that is knowing, the thoughts that speak to our wonder, that make us translucent and, as shame is consumed in wonder, transparent.

Following then the thoughts that speak to our wonder, I came to a place "in my heart where my soul dwells," the place where beloved images are kept. Here I believe I find God knowing in our knowing, for here I find the knowing that comes of loving. Actually I find the realm of beloved images, the woman playing before God in the beginning of time, the man crying out to God in the fullness of time, the child playing at the end of time. All of these are figures of the wisdom of God. All are images of the knowing that comes of loving. The insight into the image is the reality, the knowing itself. As I gain insight into image, therefore, I pass from image to reality. Meditating on the woman playing before God in the beginning of time, I pass as at Ayasofya from the image to the reality of God's eyes and heart. Meditating on the man crying out to God in the fullness of time, I pass as at Rothko from the image to the reality of the human eyes and heart of Christ. Meditating on the child playing at the end of time, I pass as in the Meditation Room from the image to the reality of my own eyes and heart. I find "indwelling soul," knowing in knowing and loving in loving, God living in us and us living in God.

A woman playing before God in the beginning of time, my first image of Holy Wisdom, and the words of promise, "my eyes and my heart will be there for all time," have been the inspiration of my pilgrimage and have led me to seek God's eyes and heart. I have thought in this way to walk "the road of the union of love with God." I have a fear, though, of deceiving myself, of falling into "that cunning semblance of love which flourishes in the imagination," as Hawthorne says, "but strikes no depth of root in the heart."[16] Still, my encounter with the wonder of existence seems real enough, the certainty "I am," though it involves imagination, looking up into a starry night; also my enounter with death, the certainty "I will die," though it too involves imagination, seeing my life open up all the way to death. The reality of love and of wisdom, of knowing that comes of loving, seems similar, where "I am" and "I will die" come together in "depth of root in the heart."

A man crying out to God in the fullness of time, my image of Christ, and the words of his cry, "My God, my God, why hast thou forsaken me?"[17] reveal to me the "depth of root in the heart" where "I am" meets "I will die." It is the relation of Jesus with God that is the reality here, a relation that endures suffering and death and survives it, a relation that endures even being forsaken by God and is expressed in the very cry, "My God, my God." Barnett Newman introducing his *Stations of the Cross*, abstract paintings like those of Mark Rothko but vertical rather than horizontal, bright rather than dark, uses the Aramaic words of the cry, *lema sabachthani*. "Why? Why did you forsake me? Why forsake me? To what purpose? Why?" he repeats. "This is the Passion," he says. "This outcry of Jesus. Not the terrible walk up the Via Dolorosa, but the question that has no answer."[18] I would say not only the terrible walk up the Via Dolorosa but also the terrible cry that gives words to the walk. Still, I find an answer in the cry itself, an answer to "why hast thou forsaken me?" in "My God, my God," an answer to suffering and death in the relation with God that endures and survives it. There is joy in that relation and life. There is joy and life in the human eyes and heart of Christ.

A child playing at the end of time, my final image, and the words of prophecy, "a little child shall lead them,"[19] seem to point then to joy and life, to beauty and golden light as I am finding at World's End, to a seeing of *apokalypsis* as "revelation" and a feeling of *parousia* as "presence." These last things are meanings I have brought here with me, to be sure, meanings of words, and yet they suggest a true seeing and a true feeling. They hint at what I have found everywhere on my pilgrimage, eyes for revelation and a heart for presence. I have learned since I came here that World's End was once a proposed site for the United Nations.[20] Imagine the UN here! Yet imagining it here is like thinking of our times in terms of what I am seeing and feeling here. If the dark of our times is that of seeing without feeling, and the cold is that of feeling without seeing, then the eyes and the heart I am using here do look and speak to our times.

Eyes for revelation and a heart for presence, these eyes can see the Four Horsemen of the Apocalypse at large in our times, war and famine and sickness and death, but this heart can feel presence at work in our times too, the presence of God and our presence, the presence of Christ in our relation with God. When "presence" to the heart is revealed to the eyes, it is "coming." That is the full meaning of *apokalypsis* and *parousia*. It is the meaning of the concluding words of the New Testament, "Come, Lord Jesus!"[21] Meanwhile, seeing conjoined with feeling, a knowing that is loving and a loving that is knowing, is aware of the presence at work in our times, like Brother Lawrence seeing the tree barren in winter and knowing it would come alive in spring. I came here to World's End with a friend who had invited me to Boston to be on a panel on nuclear war, on living in a nuclear age. The panel was called off, and so we came here instead. It seems ironic, almost as if a vision of destruction had given way to a vision of beauty and of golden light, as if the madness of our times, the terror and the despair, had given way to knowing that comes of loving.

NOTES

1. There is *A History of World's End* by William H. C. Walker and Willard Brewer Walker (Milton, Mass.: The Trustees of Reservations, 1973) with maps and photographs. World's End is mentioned a number of times in passing in Elizabeth Coatsworth's book on Hingham, *South Shore Town* (New York: Macmillan, 1948), pp. 2, 29, 56, and especially 99.

2. Genesis 3:8.
3. Cf. Willard R. Trask, *The Unwritten Song* (New York: Macmillan, 1967), 2: 252 where it is translated literally (by Washington Matthews) "Beauty before me, I walk with. Beauty behind me, I walk with . . ."
4. "The Deer's Cry," trans. Kuno Meyer, *Selections from Ancient Irish Poetry* (London: Constable, 1928), p. 27.
5. I Kings 9:3 and II Chronicles 7:16.
6. John 1:14.
7. Cf. Cyril Mango's essay on mosaics in Heinz Kähler, *Hagia Sophia*, trans. Ellyn Childs (New York: Praeger, 1967), p. 53.
8. I John 1:1.
9. W. B. Yeats, "Under Ben Bulben" in *The Collected Poems of W. B. Yeats* (New York: Macmillan, 1956), p. 344.
10. Matthew 28:20 (King James).
11. Philippians 4:7.
12. Henry David Thoreau, *Walden*, ed. J. Lyndon Shanley (Princeton, N.J.: Princeton University Press, 1971), p. 8.
13. Michael Polanyi, *The Tacit Dimension* (Garden City, N.Y.: Doubleday, 1967), p. 4.
14. Cf. the sayings where the word *secrets* occurs in the *Libre de Amic e Amat* (nos. 32, 75, 76, and 155) in Salvador Galmes and Miguel Ferra (eds.), *Obres de Ramon Lull*, vol. 9 (Palma de Mallorca: Comissio Editora Lulliana, 1914), pp. 383, 389, 390, and 400–401.
15. Nathaniel Hawthorne, "Rappacini's Daughter" in Alfred Kazin (ed.), *Selected Short Stories of Nathaniel Hawthorne* (Greenwich, Conn.: Fawcett, 1966), p. 130.
16. Ibid.
17. Matthew 27:46 (cf. Mark 15:34).
18. Barnett Newman, *The Stations of the Cross* (New York: Simon R. Guggenheim Foundation, 1966), p. 9. Cf. also the color reproductions of his stations in Harold Rosenberg, *Barnett Newman* (New York: Harry N. Abrams, 1978), pp. 150–163.
19. Isaiah 11:6.
20. Cf. Walker and Walker, *A History of World's End*, p. 51.
21. Apocalypse (Revelation) 22:20.

Index

Donne, John, 139, 145

Eckhart, Master, 3, 4, 13, 14, 18, 20, 75, 119, 124
Ecstasy, 133
Einstein, Albert, 88, 104, 107, 110
Eliot, T.S., 135
Erikson, Erik, 133
Essential Desire, 144
Eternal life, 66
Eternity, 3
Eve. *See* Adam and Eve
Evil, 73; Hammarskjold on, 125; of the heart, 99; wisdom and, 126-127
Existence is God, 14, 20, 75, 124
Extreme solitude of the heart, 96

Falstaff, 46, 47
Famine, 73, 74
Fatigue in living, 21
Faulkner, William, 74
Fears, 19
Forgetfulness, 124
Foucauld, Charles de, 15
Frankl, Viktor, 66
Freedom, 8
Future, 109

Games, 68-69
Gandhi, 4, 14, 20, 75, 124
Gelassenheit, 119
God: absorption by, 40; definition of, 12; dwells in you, 21-22; and evil, 73; existence of, 124; expectations and, 19; as infinite sphere, 45; of Islam, 37-38; Jesus' relationship to, 165; journey with, 1; is Light, 37-38; and loneliness, 52-53, 75; mercy seat for, 17; of Muslim faith, 156; necessity for, 51-52; presence of, 158; secrets of, 98; self-realization in, 95, 96; speaking with, 13; subtle but not malicious, 104-105; time of, 65-66; union of love with, 6, 11; Van Gogh and, 50; vision in death, 142; walking with, 152
The Golden Key (MacDonald), 1, 60, 70
Grand Canyon, 59
The Green Child (Read), 1, 3, 10, 60

Grounded transparently in God, 141, 144
Gunkel, Hermann, Jr., 14

Hagia Sophia, 25-54
Hamlet, 120
Hammarskjold, Dag, 4, 43, 63, 108-109, 119, 125, 126-127, 129, 130, 140-141
Hawthorne, Nathaniel, 163, 165
Heart-free, 119
Heart's ease, 129-138, 164
Heart Sutra, 140
Heidegger, Martin, 13, 119, 120
Helen of Troy, 7, 16
Heraclitus, 70
Herzog, Werner, 64
Historical inevitability, 60
Holy Spirit, 34
Holy Wisdom, 25-54
Hopes, 19

I am, 133
I and Thou (Buber), 91-92
Imagination, 2-3; of the heart, 95
Indwelling, 147
Infinite sphere images, 45, 46
Insight, 159
Intensity, simplification through, 36-37
Inward peace, 112
Isaiah, 71
Islam: call to prayer, 37; divine unity, 36; God of, 156; *see also* Koran; Muhammad
Islandia (Wright), 75

Jacob, Max, 90, 96, 110, 111, 136, 146, 161
Jealous love, 97, 98
Jesus: eternal birth of, 18; eternal life and, 66; face of the sky, 80; and Holy Wisdom, 33-34; human figure of, 3; I am the Truth, 44; I of, 133-134; in John's Gospel, 20; relationship to God, 165; Repent!, 77; in Rothko Chapel, 81-84; on wisdom, 123
John's Gospel, 19, 20; and liturgies, 28-29
Johnson, Samuel, 16
John the Baptist, 80
Joy, reality of, 86